Gourmet
VEGETARIAN FEASTS

A cornucopia of international treats to suit every taste.

for chris + Keeth,
w/ Love + Respect
to YOR HEALThs
SALUTé / ASANTé

from,

Lonney

Gourmet
VEGETARIAN FEASTS

Martha Rose Shulman

Illustrated by Elaine Hill

THORSONS PUBLISHING GROUP
Rochester, Vermont
•
Wellingborough, Northamptonshire

First published 1984 as *Garlic Cookery* and *Herb and Honey Cookery*. This revised, combined, and reset edition first published 1987

LIBRARY OF CONGRESS CATALOGING-IN-PUBLICATION DATA
Shulman, Martha Rose
   Gourmet vegetarian feasts.
   Rev. ed. of: Garlic cookery and Herb and honey
   cookery. 1984
   Includes index.
   1. Vegetarian cookery. 2. Cookery (Garlic)
3. Cookery (Herbs) 4. Cookery (Honey)
   I. Shulman, Martha Rose. Garlic cookery.
   II. Shulman, Martha Rose. Herb and honey cookery.
   III. Title.
   TX837.S4679 1987   641.6'5   86-30054
   ISBN 0-7225-1407-7 (pbk.)

Printed and bound in the United States

10   9   8   7   6   5   4   3   2   1

Distributed to the book trade in the United States by Harper & Row Publishers, Inc.

Distributed to the book trade in Canada by the Book Center, Inc., Montreal, Quebec

Distributed to the health food trade in Canada by Alive Books, Toronto and Vancouver

CONTENTS

INTRODUCTION

Here is a collection of delicious gourmet vegetarian dishes based on the cuisines of many different countries. Most of the recipes include garlic, herbs or honey — natural foods that have been used for thousands of years to add individuality and subtle flavors to wholefood cooking as well as helping digestion. All the recipes are vegetarian and except in the chapter on vegan main course dishes, dairy produce and eggs are often used in a range of dishes which delight both eye and palate.

Show off at your next party with a feast of these dishes assembled to impress guests. Make everyday meals memorable with vegetarian recipes that are utterly delicious and sharp on style. The new vegetarian approach to eating is light years away from the earnest, more humble foods of earlier days and there are few hard and fast rules on what to serve and when. Many of the appetizers would be equally acceptable at a weekend brunch, the salad and side dishes would make light lunches and the soups, breads and spreads be perfect for informally sophisticated suppers. However simple the feast, make it more special and present it with flair — a soup-of-the-day in an attractive tureen; a pasta supper served on a pretty cotton-print tablecloth; a salad garnished with nasturtium flowers. These are the imaginative touches, inexpensive in themselves, which transform meals into feasts that are memorable social occasions of the warmest kind, spiced with good food and good fellowship.

1
BREAKFASTS

COUSCOUS WITH HONEY AND FRUIT

Serves 4

1. Place couscous in a bowl and pour on the water. Let sit 10 to 15 minutes, or until soft.
2. Heat the butter in a frying pan and add apple and pear. Sauté a few minutes, then add water or apple juice, honey, raisins and spices. Cook, stirring, over medium heat, 3 to 5 minutes.
3. Stir in couscous and heat through, stirring. Remove from heat and serve, topping with yogurt, and if you wish, additional honey.

1 cup couscous
2 cups water
1 tablespoon butter
1 apple, cored and chopped
1 pear, cored and chopped
3 tablespoons water or apple juice
1 tablespoon honey
4 tablespoons raisins
1 teaspoon ground cinnamon
½ teaspoon freshly grated nutmeg
Plain low-fat yogurt and additional honey for topping

MINTED BREAKFAST DRINK

A marvelous, refreshing drink to wake up to.

Makes 1 drink

1 cup freshly squeezed
    orange juice
2 tablespoons fresh mint
Handful of alfalfa sprouts
½ ripe banana
2 ice cubes

1. Place all the ingredients in a blender and blend until smooth. Drink at once.

OATMEAL WITH FRUIT AND HONEY

Serves 3

2 cups water
2 tablespoons mild honey
Pinch of sea salt
1 cup rolled oats
3 tablespoons raisins
½-1 teaspoon ground
    cinnamon
½ teaspoon freshly grated
    nutmeg
1 apple, grated and tossed
    with juice of ½ lemon
Warm milk for topping
Additional cinnamon
    (optional)

1. Place water in a saucepan, add honey and salt and bring to a rolling boil.
2. Slowly pour in rolled oats, stirring all the while with a wooden spoon. Add raisins, cinnamon and nutmeg, bring to a second boil, and reduce heat. Cover and simmer 15 to 20 minutes, or until liquid is absorbed.
3. Top each serving with grated apple, warm milk, and if you wish, additional cinnamon.

PAIN PERDU (FRENCH TOAST)

*French toast is traditionally made with stale brioche, the
French solution to leftover bread. I often use day-old
challah (see recipe page 151), but you can really use any
bread, and it doesn't have to be stale. It should end up
crisp on the outside and soft and custardy on the inside.
The honey you use can be strong or mild.*

Serves 6

1. Slice bread an hour or two before you make the
   French toast, if you can, so that it will dry out.
2. Put oven on low (unless intending to serve as
   soon as cooked). Beat eggs with milk and stir in
   vanilla, honey, cinnamon, nutmeg, optional
   orange flower water, and salt. Heat butter in a
   large, heavy frying pan over low heat.
3. Dip bread slices into batter on both sides. They
   should be saturated but not so soggy that they fall
   apart. Place in frying pan and continue dipping
   slices and adding them to pan (but don't
   overcrowd the pan). Sauté slowly, until the first
   side turns golden brown, about 5 to 7 minutes.
   Then turn and sauté on the other side until
   golden brown. Place in oven on a baking sheet to
   keep warm if you aren't serving at once. Serve
   with honey.

*1 loaf challah or other
  bread, cut in ¾-inch
  slices
3 large eggs
1 cup milk
¾ teaspoon vanilla extract
1 tablespoon honey
Pinch of cinnamon
Pinch of freshly grated
  nutmeg
1 teaspoon orange flower
  water (optional)
Small pinch of sea salt
Unsalted butter for
  sautéing, as needed
Additional honey for
  topping*

SEMOLINA WITH RAISINS AND CINNAMON

Serves 4

2 ½ cups water
¼ teaspoon sea salt
1 cup semolina or cream of
  wheat
1 teaspoon cinnamon
4 tablespoons raisins
1 cup Honeyed Yogurt
  Cereal Topping
(page 16)

1. Bring water to a boil in a saucepan. Add salt, and slowly pour in semolina in a very thin stream, stirring all the time with a wooden spoon.
2. Add sea salt, cinnamon, and raisins, bring to a second boil, reduce heat, and cover. Cook 15 minutes, or until liquid is absorbed.
3. Serve, topping each bowl with a generous amount of Honeyed Yogurt Cereal Topping.

MIXED GRAINS MUESLI

Makes 3 servings

1 cup water
1 cup milk (or use all water)
Pinch of sea salt
½ cup rolled oats
½ cup wheat flakes
2 tablespoons bran
1 teaspoon cinnamon
3 tablespoons raisins
½ apple, grated or finely
  chopped
½ pear, grated or finely
  chopped
2-4 tablespoons toasted
  wheat germ
1 tablespoon honey
Additional warm milk to
  taste
2 tablespoons broken
  pecans or chopped
hazelnuts

1. Bring water and milk to a boil in a 1 quart saucepan. Add a little salt.
2. Combine oats, wheat, bran, and cinnamon, stirring all the while with a wooden spoon; add this very slowly to boiling liquid. Stir in raisins and when liquid reaches a second boil, cover, reduce heat, and simmer gently 15 minutes, or until liquid is absorbed.
3. Spoon into bowls and top with wheat germ, grated apples and pears, honey, and pecans. Add warm milk to taste.

FANCY GRANOLA

If you make this large amount you'll only have to make granola once a month or even less — unless of course you find it so good (as you undoubtedly will) that you also eat it for snacks. This makes a nice gift as well as an important family staple.

Enough to fill a gallon jar

1. Preheat oven to 325°F.
2. In a large bowl mix together all the dry ingredients except raisins. Add vanilla and milk.
3. Heat honey and oil together over low heat in a saucepan, just until they blend together easily. Pour mixture over granola and stir and fold in so that all the grains are coated. Make sure that no part of the mixture is dry, or granola won't bake evenly.
4. Oil or butter two large baking pans and spoon in granola. The layers should not be more than 1½ inches thick. Place in oven and set timer for 15 minutes. Stir mixture and set for another 15 minutes. Stir again. After 45 minutes granola should be brown (it may be done a little sooner, so check carefully after the first 30 minutes). Now stir in raisins and turn off heat. Leave oven door ajar and let cool in oven.
5. When granola is completely cool, spoon into jars or plastic bags. If possible, store in refrigerator.

3 cups rolled oats
1½ cups flaked wheat
1½ cups flaked rye
3 cups raw wheat germ
1 cup soy flour
¼ cup powdered milk
1 teaspoon sea salt
1 tablespoon cinnamon
2 teaspoons nutmeg
⅔ cup sunflower seeds
⅔ cup chopped almonds
⅔ cup cashews
⅔ cup sesame seeds, cracked in a blender
⅔ cup grated or shaved coconut
2 tablespoons vanilla extract
¼ cup milk
¾ cup safflower oil
1 cup mild honey
2 cups raisins

STRAWBERRY OMELETTE

This may sound unlikely, but it's one of the most special breakfasts I can think of. Makes a particularly memorable breakfast in bed.

For each omelette:

1 tablespoon butter for pan
2 eggs, beaten
A generous handful of
    stemmed strawberries
2 tablespoons plain yogurt
1 teaspoon mild honey
Fresh mint for garnish

1. Heat butter in an omelette pan, and meanwhile beat eggs.
2. Crush strawberries very slightly and mix together with yogurt and honey.
3. When butter has stopped sizzling, pour in eggs and tilt pan to coat evenly. Gently shake pan while lifting edges of omelette so that uncooked eggs can run underneath. As soon as it is set, spread strawberry mixture down the center.
4. Fold omelette, cook a minute longer, and turn out of pan onto a plate. Garnish with fresh mint and serve.

YOGURT PANCAKES

Makes 18 pancakes

2 eggs, separated
1 tablespoon honey
1 cup plain yogurt
1 tablespoon melted butter
    or safflower oil
1 ½ cups sifted whole
    wheat pastry flour
Pinch of sea salt
1 teaspoon baking powder
Oil for sautéing
Honey for topping

1. Beat together egg yolks, honey, yogurt, and melted butter or safflower oil.
2. Sift together flour, salt, and baking powder.
3. Stir egg yolk mixture into flour mixture.
4. Beat egg whites until they form stiff, shiny peaks. Gently fold into batter.
5. Heat a heavy, wide frying pan over medium-high heat and brush with oil. Drop batter in by heaping tablespoons. Cook on the first side until bubbles break through, turn (it should be golden brown), and cook until golden brown on the other side. Serve warm, with honey.

BUCKWHEAT PANCAKES

Makes 18 pancakes

1. Beat together egg yolks, honey, milk, and melted butter or safflower oil.
2. Sift together whole wheat pastry flour and buckwheat flour, sea salt, and baking powder.
3. Stir egg yolk mixture into flour mixture.
4. Beat egg whites until they form stiff, shiny peaks. Gently fold into batter.
5. Heat a heavy, wide frying pan over medium-high heat and brush with oil. Drop in heaping tablespoons of batter. Cook on the first side until bubbles break through, turn (it should be golden brown), and cook until golden brown on the other side. Serve warm, with honey.

2 eggs, separated
2 tablespoons honey*
1 cup milk
1 tablespoon melted butter or safflower oil
¾ cup sifted whole wheat pastry flour
¾ cup sifted buckwheat flour
¼ teaspoon sea salt
1 teaspoon baking powder
Oil for sautéing
Honey for topping

* You can use mild or strong honey. Buckwheat honey, which is dark and strong, would give these a pronounced buckwheat flavor. Experiment with different kinds.

HONEYED YOGURT CEREAL TOPPING

Try this for a change on hot cereal or granola.

1 cup plain low-fat yogurt
1 tablespoon mild honey
½ ripe banana
½ teaspoon vanilla extract
·Pinch of nutmeg

1. Blend together all ingredients in a blender or food processor until smooth. Refrigerate until ready to use.

BRAIDED FRUIT-FILLED COFFEE CAKE

For the dough:
1 tablespoon active dry
    yeast
½ cup lukewarm water
½ cup orange juice
4 tablespoons mild honey
1 egg, beaten
4 tablespoons powdered
    milk
1 tablespoon grated orange
    rind
2½ cups unbleached white
    flour
3 tablespoons melted butter
    or safflower oil
1 teaspoon sea salt
1½ cups whole wheat flour
Additional unbleached
    white flour for kneading

1. Prepare dough. Dissolve yeast in water in a large bowl. Heat orange juice in a small pan and stir in honey, then remove from heat and cool to lukewarm. Add to yeast mixture. Stir in egg, powdered milk, and orange rind. Stir in ⅔ cup of the unbleached white flour and stir 100 times for the sponge. Cover and set in a warm place 1 hour.
2. Fold in butter or oil and salt. Fold in whole wheat flour and remaining unbleached white flour. Flour kneading surface and turn out dough. Knead 10 to 15 minutes, until smooth and elastic, adding flour as necessary. Wash out the bowl, oil it, and place dough in it. Cover and let rise in a warm place 1 hour.
3. Meanwhile prepare the filling. Combine water and dried fruit in a saucepan and simmer over medium heat, adding water if necessary, until fruit is softened. Combine with all the other filling ingredients except honey in a large bowl, and toss together well.

4. Punch down dough and turn out onto your work surface. Roll into a rectangle about 16 inches long and 12 inches wide. Brush with honey, and spread filling down the center third of rectangle. Now, using a sharp knife, cut dough on either side into 1-inch strips pointed in a downward angle.
5. Fold strips in over filling, alternating sides so that you are weaving one over the other like a braid. When you get to the end, pinch braids over lower end. Carefully transfer coffee cake to a lightly oiled baking sheet. Let rise 40 minutes while you preheat oven to 350°F.
6. Brush braid with egg wash, sprinkle with slivered almonds, and brush again with egg wash. Place in preheated oven and bake 30 to 40 minutes, or until golden brown.
7. While coffee cake is baking, combine remaining honey with water in a saucepan and heat together. When you remove coffee cake from oven, brush with this mixture.
8. Serve warm.

For the filling:
¼ cup water, plus more as needed
½ cup chopped, dried fruit
2 peaches, peeled and sliced
3 plums, sliced
2 apples, sliced
1 banana, sliced
½ cup chopped almonds
1 teaspoon ground cinnamon
¼ teaspoon freshly grated nutmeg
1 tablespoon grated orange rind
1 teaspoon vanilla extract
4 tablespoons mild honey

For the topping:
1 egg, beaten with 4 tablespoons water
½ cup slivered almonds
4-8 tablespoons mild honey
½ cup

DARK HONEY CAKE

2 tablespoons halved
   almonds
1 cup sifted unbleached
   white flour
1½ cups sifted whole
   wheat pastry flour
1½ teaspoons cinnamon
½ teaspoon freshly grated
   nutmeg
½ teaspoon ground
   cardamom
¼ teaspoon ground ginger
¼ teaspoon ground cloves
2 teaspoons baking soda
Pinch of sea salt
4 ounces butter
1 cup dark honey
6 eggs, separated
Grated rind of 1 lemon
½ cup milk

1. Preheat oven to 375°F. Butter a 10-inch tube pan or a spring form pan and sprinkle almonds over the bottom.
2. Sift together flours, spices, baking soda, and sea salt.
3. Cream together butter and honey. Add egg yolks and lemon rind.
4. Add flour mixture in batches, alternating with milk and ending with flour, to butter mixture, beating between additions.
5. Beat egg whites until stiff but not dry, and carefully fold into batter. Pour batter into prepared cake pan and place in preheated oven. Bake 40 minutes. Reduce heat to 325°F and bake another 20 to 30 minutes, or until a cake tester comes out clean. Cool 10 minutes in the pan, then carefully turn out onto a rack and cool. Wrap well and store for a few days before cutting.

SCONES

Makes 24

1. Preheat oven to 400°F. Butter two baking sheets.
2. Beat together yogurt or milk, egg, and honey in a large bowl. Sift together flour, baking powder, baking soda, and sea salt. Stir ⅔ of flour mixture into milk mixture, a cup at a time, and mix well. Gradually add melted butter, mixing in well. Stir in currants, orange peel, and remaining flour. Mix together with hands or a wooden spoon until dough is stiff enough to knead. Add a little more flour if necessary.
3. Turn out onto a lightly floured board and knead about 10 times, just until ingredients are combined. Divide dough into 4 equal pieces and press out each piece into a thick circle about 5 to 6 inches in diameter. Cut each circle into quarters and place on baking sheets.
4. Bake 15 to 20 minutes, or until just beginning to brown on top. Serve warm with butter, honey, or preserves.

1 cup yogurt or sour milk or buttermilk
1 egg
3 tablespoons mild honey
3 cups whole wheat pastry flour
2 teaspoons baking powder
1 teaspoon baking soda
½ teaspoon sea salt
⅓ cup melted butter
½ cup currants
1½ tablespoons grated orange peel

OMELETTE AUX FINES HERBES

1 tablespoon butter
2 eggs
1 teaspoon milk
Sea salt and freshly ground
  black pepper
1 heaping tablespoon fines
  herbes (parsley, chives,
  thyme, basil, or
  tarragon)
1 sliver garlic, chopped
Additional herbs for
  garnish (optional)

1. Heat butter in omelette pan, and meanwhile beat eggs together with milk and a little sea salt and freshly ground pepper.
2. When butter stops sizzling, pour in eggs. Keep shaking and tilting the pan with one hand as you gently lift the edges of the omelette with a spatula with the other hand, so that eggs on top can run underneath.
3. As soon as bottom of omelette is set, spread herbs and garlic down the center. Turn omelette and cook another half a minute or so, or until eggs are no longer runny. Turn out onto a plate and serve, garnishing with more herbs if you wish.

MUSHROOM AND CHEESE OMELETTE

Serves 2 to 3

2 tablespoons butter
½ pound mushrooms,
  cleaned, trimmed, and
  sliced thin
1 clove garlic, minced or
  put through a press
¼ teaspoon thyme
¼ teaspoon crushed
  rosemary
1 tablespoon dry white
  wine
Salt and freshly ground
  black pepper, to taste
4 eggs, beaten
1 teaspoon milk
½ cup grated Gruyère or
  Parmesan cheese
Fresh chopped parsley, for
  garnish

1. Heat half the butter in a frying pan and add mushrooms and garlic.
2. Cook over moderate heat 5 minutes, or until mushrooms begin to soften.
3. Add thyme, rosemary, and white wine and continue to sauté another 5 minutes, or until liquid evaporates.
4. Season to taste with salt and freshly ground pepper, remove from heat, and set aside.
5. Heat remaining butter in an omelette pan, and beat eggs and milk in a bowl. Make omelette as instructed in the Tomato Omelette (opposite), filling with sautéed mushrooms and grated cheese. Turn onto a platter or plates, garnish with parsley, and serve.

TOMATO OMELETTE

Serves 2 to 3

1. Heat half the butter in a frying pan and add tomatoes and garlic. Cook together 15 minutes over medium heat.
2. Season to taste with salt and freshly ground pepper and add chopped fresh basil or tarragon. Remove from heat.
3. Heat rest of butter in an omelette pan while you beat eggs in a bowl. Beat in teaspoon of milk and a little salt and pepper.
4. As soon as butter stops sizzling, pour eggs into omelette pan and swirl pan. Shake pan gently as you lift edges of omelette and allow eggs to run underneath.
5. When omelette is solid enough to fold, place tomatoes in a line down the center and fold omelette, either by jerking pan quickly away from you then towards you, so that eggs flip over, or by folding with a spatula, whichever is the more comfortable for you.
6. Cook a few more minutes, depending on how runny you like your omelettes, and turn out onto a warm serving dish.
7. This can also be made in two batches in a smaller omelette pan and turned out directly onto the plates.

2 tablespoons butter
¾ pound tomatoes, seeded and chopped
1 clove garlic, minced or put through a press
Sea salt and freshly ground black pepper, to taste
1 teaspoon chopped fresh basil or tarragon
4 eggs, beaten
1 teaspoon milk

2

APPETIZERS

SPINACH PÂTÉ

Serves 6

3 pounds fresh spinach,
  washed and stems
  removed, or 3 pounds
  frozen, thawed
1 tablespoon butter
½ onion, minced
2 cloves garlic, minced or
  put through a press
1 teaspoon thyme
1 teaspoon oregano
1 tablespoon wine or cider
  vinegar
3 eggs
½ cup skim milk
⅛ teaspoon freshly grated
  nutmeg
4 tablespoons chopped
  fresh parsley
½ cup freshly grated
  Parmesan cheese
½ cup freshly grated
  Gruyère cheese
¾ cup whole wheat
  breadcrumbs
Sea salt, to taste
Freshly ground black
  pepper

1. Preheat oven to 350°F. Butter a loaf pan or pâté terrine and line with buttered waxed paper.
2. If using frozen spinach, thaw, squeeze out all the moisture and chop very fine, almost to a purée. If using fresh spinach, wash and stem, heat a large non-aluminum pan or wok, and add the still wet spinach in batches. Cook in its own liquid just until it wilts. Cool under cold water and squeeze out all the moisture. Chop fine, almost to a purée.
3. Heat butter in a heavy-bottomed pan and sauté minced onion until tender. Add garlic, spinach, thyme, oregano, and vinegar and cook, stirring, 3 to 5 minutes. Add more butter if necessary. Remove from heat.
4. Beat eggs together with milk and stir in spinach mixture along with remaining ingredients. Adjust seasonings and spoon into prepared baking pan. Smooth top and cover with a piece of buttered waxed paper. Cover with foil or a lid and bake for 45 minutes in a preheated oven, or until the top just begins to brown.
5. Remove from the heat, cool and unmold. This is good served with Tomato Coulis (page 136). You can also garnish it with slices of hard-boiled egg. It freezes well.

Artichokes à la Grecque

Serves 4 to 6

1. Combine all ingredients for bouillon in a large flame-proof casserole or stock pot and bring to a simmer. Simmer, covered, while you prepare artichokes (10 to 15 minutes).
2. To trim artichoke bottoms, cut stems off and rub with lemon juice. Starting at base of artichoke, break off all the leaves by bending them backward.
3. Trim all the leaves around the bottom of the artichoke like this until you reach the part where the artichoke begins to curve inwards.
4. Cut off remaining leaves with a sharp knife. Rub continuously with lemon juice so that artichokes will not discolor.
5. Now trim the bottom of the artichoke by rotating against the sharp blade of a knife, so that all the tough green skin is cut away and the white fleshy part underneath the leaves is exposed. Rub cut surfaces with lemon juice and drop in a bowl of water acidulated with the juice of 1 lemon.
6. When all of the artichoke bottoms are prepared, drop into simmering bouillon. Simmer, covered, 30 to 40 minutes, or until tender. Remove from heat and allow to cool in marinade.
7. Remove chokes by carefully pulling apart at the center and scooping out with a spoon. Refrigerate artichoke bottoms in marinade for 2 hours, or overnight.
8. Drain off marinade, discard parsley and bay leaf, and place marinade in a saucepan. Reduce over high heat to ½ cup. Adjust seasonings.
9. Place artichoke bottoms on a platter or on individual plates and pour on reduced bouillon. Garnish with fresh chervil or parsley and serve.

For the bouillon/marinade:
2 cups water
1 cup dry white wine
Juice of 2 large lemons
2 tablespoons vinegar
½ cup olive oil
2 cloves garlic
12 black peppercorns
1 tablespoon coriander seeds
1 bay leaf
4 sprigs parsley
½ teaspoon mustard seeds
1 teaspoon fennel seeds
1 branch fennel (optional)
½ teaspoon sea salt
1 large shallot, chopped
⅔ cup raisins

For the artichokes:
4 to 6 large globe artichokes
1 cut lemon
10 to 12 sprigs chervil or 1 tablespoon chopped fresh parsley

CHIVE CRÊPES

These crêpes can also be made with other herbs. Try them with chervil, parsley, dill, or a mixture. They can be filled or served as a side dish.

Makes about 24 crêpes

4 eggs
1 cup milk
1 cup water
½ teaspoon sea salt (more
    to taste)
1 cup sifted unbleached
    white flour
1 cup sifted whole wheat
    pastry flour
4 tablespoons melted butter
6 tablespoons minced
    chives
Freshley ground black
    pepper (optional)
Butter for the pan

1. Place eggs, milk, water, and sea salt in blender jar and turn on blender. While blender is running add flours and melted butter. Blend at high speed 1 minute. Transfer to a bowl and refrigerate 2 hours, covered.
2. Stir chives into crêpe batter.
3. Heat a crêpe pan or 6- to 8-inch omelette pan (a cast iron crêpe pan is preferable) over a medium-high flame and brush with butter. Just when butter begins to smoke, lift pan from heat and ladle in about 3 tablespoons crêpe batter. Swirl pan as soon as you pour in batter, to coat evenly (don't be too upset if you don't get this right at first, or if there are holes in the crêpe). Return to heat and cook crêpe about 1 to 1½ minutes. Shake pan to loosen crêpe, or lift gently with a butter knife or spatula. I usually loosen crêpe by sliding a butter knife all the way around the edge, then lift crêpe with my fingers. Don't force crêpe; if it sticks, it isn't ready to turn. It should be golden brown and come away from the pan easily. Turn crêpe and cook about 30 seconds on the other side. Turn out onto a plate.
4. You shouldn't have to butter the crêpe pan between each crêpe after the first one or two. I usually add a little butter after about 5 crêpes, just a small amount, on the end of a brush or a paper towel. Continue to make crêpes until you use up all the batter.
5. If serving crêpes plain, brush with a small amount of herb butter or unsalted plain butter, fold in half with the second side you cooked (the less cooked side) on the *inside* and the pretty

brown side on the outside, and fold in half again, to make a kind of triangle. Place in a buttered baking dish, cover and keep in a warm oven until ready to serve. Or fill with the filling of your choice (ratatouille, creamed spinach, cheese, cheese and egg, leftover vegetables, etc.), roll up, and heat through in a medium oven.

Note: If not using right away, store by stacking between pieces of waxed paper to prevent sticking. Wrap in a plastic bag, or in plastic and foil, and refrigerate or freeze.

HOMMOS (MIDDLE EASTERN CHICKPEA PURÉE)

Serves 6 to 8

1. Combine chickpeas with 5 cups water in a large pot, bring to a boil, reduce heat, and simmer 1 hour.
2. Add ½ to 1 teaspoon salt and continue to simmer another hour, until chickpeas are soft. Drain, retaining some of the liquid.
3. In a blender, food processor, or mortar and pestle grind together cooked chickpeas, lemon juice, garlic, olive oil, tahini, and yogurt until you have a smooth paste. Add more yogurt or some cooking liquid from beans if you want a smoother purée. Add salt to taste and ground cumin, and blend in.
4. Transfer to a bowl, sprinkle with parsley, and garnish with black olives. Serve with bread, crackers, or rounds of cucumber. This can be frozen.

1 cup chickpeas, washed, picked over, and soaked for several hours or overnight in three times their volume water
Sea salt, to taste
¼ - ½ cup lemon juice, or to taste
2 large cloves garlic
¼ cup good olive oil
6-8 heaping tablespoons tahini
6-8 tablespoons plain low-fat yogurt
½ teaspoon ground cumin
Freshly chopped parsley for garnish
Halved black olives for garnish

SWEET AND SOUR LEEKS

Serves 4

2 tablespoons safflower oil
3 cloves garlic, minced
1 tablespoon mild honey
2 tablespoons dry white
    wine
1-2 tablespoons tomato
    paste, to taste
16 small leeks, white part
    only, sliced about 1 inch
    thick
3 sprigs fresh thyme
2 tablespoons lemon juice
Sea salt and freshly ground
    black pepper

1. Heat oil in a heavy, wide frying pan and add
    garlic. Sauté about 3 minutes, until golden, and
    add honey and white wine. Stir together well and
    add tomato paste. Cook together for a few
    seconds, and stir in leeks.
2. Cook leeks over medium heat, stirring, about 3
    minutes. Add thyme and lemon juice, reduce
    heat, cover, and cook gently 10 to 15 minutes,
    stirring from time to time. If pan begins to dry
    out, add a little wine or water. Add sea salt and
    freshly ground pepper to taste and remove from
    heat. Serve warm or at room temperature.

CHARCOAL-ROASTED WHOLE GARLIC

*This is especially nice if you happen to be grilling something
else. All you do is throw the prepared garlic on the coals.*

Serves 4

2 whole heads garlic (or
    more, to taste)
Olive oil

1. Brush heads of garlic with olive oil and place
    directly on hot coals of a fire that is no longer
    flaming. (You can baste the garlic a few times, but
    I find this unnecessary.)
2. When they are brown, or even charred, remove
    from fire and allow to cool. The skins will be hard
    and perhaps blackened, but inside the flesh will
    be tender.
3. Break off cloves and push out garlic. Serve on
    bread or just by itself as a side dish.

SOFT-BOILED EGGS WITH FINES HERBES

1. Bring a pot of water to a boil. Carefully lower eggs into water. Simmer 5 minutes. Remove from pot and run under cold water for about 30 seconds.
2. Clip tops off eggs using a knife or egg cutter. Stand them in egg cups. Lightly salt and pepper if you wish, and sprinkle a teaspoon of herbs over the top of the egg yolk.
3. Serve at once, with toast, and urge eaters to stir the herbs into the yolks.

1-2 eggs per person
Sea salt and freshly ground black pepper to taste
Chopped fresh basil and parsley or tarragon and parsley

CURRIED LENTIL PÂTÉ

Serves 6

1. Heat vegetable or peanut oil in a heavy-bottomed saucepan or soup pot and add onion, garlic, and spices and sauté gently until onion is tender, adding more oil if necessary.
2. Add lentils and water, bring to a boil, add salt, cover, reduce heat, and simmer 1 hour or until tender. Add more liquid if necessary. Remove from heat and drain.
3. Preheat oven to 400°F
4. Purée lentils in a blender or food processor with remaining ingredients. Adjust seasonings and pour into a buttered pâté terrine or casserole. Cover and bake 50-60 minutes. Cool and refrigerate, or serve warm. This can be frozen.

2 tablespoons safflower or peanut oil
1 medium onion, chopped
2 cloves garlic, minced or put through a press
2 teaspoons curry powder
¼ teaspoon turmeric
¼ teaspoon chili powder
½ teaspoon cumin seeds
1 cup dried lentils, washed and picked over
2-2½ cups water
1 teaspoon sea salt
2 eggs
¼ cup milk
¼ teaspoon ground ginger or ½ teaspoon grated fresh ginger
Freshly ground black pepper, to taste

SCRAMBLED EGGS
WITH CHIVES

*This is one of the simplest and best ways to enjoy chives.
The trick with scrambled eggs is to cook them slowly, over
very low heat, so that they become custardy rather than
hard. It is easy to produce creamy scrambled eggs without
any cream and with very little butter.*

Serves 4

1-2 tablespoons butter
8 eggs, beaten
*Sea salt and freshly ground
    black pepper*
*2-4 tablespoons chopped
    chives, to taste*

1. Melt butter over very low heat in a wide frying
    pan as you beat eggs about 30 times in a bowl.
    Add salt, pepper, and chives to the eggs.
2. Add eggs to pan. Stir gently over low heat.
    Nothing will happen for the first few minutes,
    then they will begin to stick to the bottom of the
    pan. Keep stirring eggs up from the bottom of the
    pan, and continue to cook and stir until eggs
    reach the desired consistency. Take the pan off
    the heat from time to time so that eggs do not
    cook too fast.
3. As soon as you see that the eggs have reached the
    consistency you want, transfer them to warm
    plates or a serving dish. They will continue to
    cook in the pan, so you might remove them from
    the heat just a second or two before you think
    they are done. Serve at once.

BAKED AND ROASTED GARLIC

Friends were somewhat hesitant the first time I served this dish, but they followed my example, squeezed their garlic onto croûtons, and were pleasantly surprised by how mild and delightful it had become. Just as in garlic soup, the garlic is mollified by the cooking. It becomes an unctious, satisfying spread and a healthy substitute for butter. This can be made in two different ways. The heads can be left whole and baked in the foil, or the cloves can be separated. It depends on how much you want to serve and in what fashion. I like the drama of the entire heads, but it's also nice to serve individual cloves.

Serves 6

1. Preheat oven to 325°F. Either separate cloves of garlic or leave heads whole, according to your taste.
2. Cut three squares of aluminum foil, double thickness if thin, large enough to thoroughly enclose one head of garlic. Place a head on each square and drizzle on oil or rub with butter. Add a little salt and pepper and thyme.
3. Seal garlic in foil. The edges should be tightly sealed, but there should be some space around the garlic so that it can expand a bit and simmer in its own juices.
4. Bake in preheated oven 1 hour. Remove from foil packages. I usually place the heads on a platter with croûtons and other crudités, and let my guests separate the cloves and squeeze the garlic out onto their bread or crudités.

3 heads fresh garlic
3 tablespoons olive oil or butter
3 sprigs thyme, or ¼ teaspoon dried thyme
Sea salt and freshly ground black pepper

TAPENADE: PROVENÇAL OLIVE PASTE

This makes a very special hors d'oeuvre spread thinly on croûtons. Serve it on a warm summer night with a glass of cool champagne or dry white or rosé wine, and let it transport you to the South of France. Traditionally tapenade is made with anchovies and tuna, but I think this is a robust and satisfying version. It is very salty and high in fat, so eat it sparingly. It is not an everyday food.

Serves 6

½ pound imported Provençal olives (Use Greek if these cannot be found.)
1-2 cloves garlic, to taste, puréed or put through a press
2 tablespoons capers
¼ teaspoon thyme (or more, to taste)
¼ teaspoon crushed rosemary (or more, to taste)
2 tablespoons olive oil
2 tablespoons lemon juice
1 teaspoon Dijon mustard
Lots of freshly ground black pepper
2 tablespoons cognac (optional)

1. Pit olives and mash to a purée with garlic and capers, using a mortar and pestle.
2. Blend in herbs, lemon juice, and olive oil and continue to mash until you have a smooth purée.
3. Blend in remaining ingredients and correct seasonings. Chill in a covered bowl until ready to serve.

CAPONATA PROVENÇAL

Serves 6 to 8

1. Preheat oven to 450°F. Pierce eggplant several times with a sharp knife, brush with olive oil, and bake 20 minutes. Remove from oven, allow to cool; peel and chop.
2. Heat olive oil in a heavy-bottomed frying pan and sauté onion, garlic, and pepper over medium-low heat about 10 minutes.
3. Add eggplant and sauté another 10 minutes, stirring from time to time and adding oil if necessary.
4. Add olives, capers, vinegar, tomatoes, salt, and freshly ground pepper and continue to cook slowly, stirring occasionally, 20 minutes. Adjust seasonings and stir in basil.
5. Remove from heat and cool. Place in a serving dish, decorate with and strips of red pepper or pimiento and lemon peel. Sprinkle with fresh parsley and chill at least an hour.
6. To serve, surround with wedges of green and red pepper and small leaves of romaine lettuce for scooping, and have a basket of croûtons or crackers close by.

2 pounds eggplant
2 tablespoons olive oil
1 small white onion, sliced thin
2 large cloves garlic, minced or put through a press
1 red or green pepper, chopped
10 green olives, pits removed, cut in half
2 tablespoons capers, rinsed
4 tablespoons red wine vinegar (or more, to taste)
3 large ripe tomatoes, peeled and chopped
Sea salt and freshly ground black pepper, to taste
1 tablespoon chopped fresh basil

For garnish:
½ red pepper or 1 pimiento, cut in thin strips
Thin strips of lemon peel
Chopped fresh parsley

For serving:
Wide strips of green and red pepper
Small leaves of romaine lettuce
Whole wheat Croûtons (page 44) or crackers

32

EGGPLANT PURÉE I: PROVENÇAL

Serves 4 to 6

3 pounds eggplant, cut in
   half lengthwise and
   scored with a sharp
   knife
2 cloves garlic, puréed or
   put through a press
2 tablespoons olive oil
Juice of 1 large lemon
2 tablespoons plain low-fat
   yogurt (optional)
Sea salt and freshly ground
   black pepper, to taste
1 tablespoon chopped fresh
   parsley or basil

1. *For a roasted or broiled taste:* Heat broiler, turning it
   as low as possible. Brush eggplant with olive oil,
   place under broiler and cook 40 to 50 minutes,
   turning once, or until completely charred and
   soft.
2. *To bake:* Preheat oven to 450°F. Place eggplant cut
   side down on an oiled baking sheet and cook 30
   minutes, or until completely soft and shrivelled.
3. Allow eggplant to cool and scoop out flesh.
   Discard skins and charred layer of cut surface.
4. Purée eggplant through a food mill, in a food
   processor, or in a mortar and pestle. Add
   remaining ingredients and mix well. Taste and
   adjust salt and pepper. You may even want to
   add more garlic!

EGGPLANT PURÉE II: WITH YOGURT AND MINT

1. Use the ingredients in the Provençal Eggplant
   Purée above, but omit olive oil and increase
   yogurt by 1 to 2 tablespoons, to taste.
2. Omit parsley or basil and substitute 1 to 2
   tablespoons chopped fresh mint, to taste.

EGGPLANT PURÉE III:
BABA GANOUCH

Serves 4 to 6

1. Grill or bake eggplant as in Eggplant Purée I.
2. Remove skins, discard seeds, and mash to a purée in a blender, food processor, or through a food mill.
3. Stir in lemon juice, garlic, yogurt, and tahini, and add salt to taste. Place in a bowl and garnish with chopped fresh parsley.
4. Surround bowl with red and green pepper strips, cucumber, carrot and celery sticks, crackers, and bread. Use vegetables to dip or spread purée on bread or crackers.

2 pounds eggplant
Juice of 1-2 lemons, to taste
1-2 cloves garlic, to taste
4 tablespoons plain low-fat yogurt
4 tablespoons tahini
Sea salt, to taste
Freshly chopped parsley for garnish

For serving:
Wide strips of red and/or green pepper
Cucumber sticks
Carrot and celery sticks
Crackers
Sliced whole wheat bread or Croûtons (page 44)

GARLIC ROQUEFORT DIP OR SPREAD

Serves 6

½ pound sharp Cheddar
   cheese, grated
½ pound Roquefort cheese
1 cup cottage cheese
4 tablespoons dry white
   wine
1 tablespoon finely chopped
   scallion, shallot or
   chives
1 clove garlic, minced or
   put through a press

1. Grate Cheddar into a mixing bowl and crumble in Roquefort. Add cottage cheese and blend thoroughly, using a wooden spoon, mixer, or food processor.
2. Add remaining ingredients and mix well. Place in a covered bowl and refrigerate until ready to use. Serve as a dip or spread.

CUCUMBERS FILLED WITH HERBED COTTAGE CHEESE

Serves 6

2 large or 3 medium
   cucumbers
1½ cups low-fat cottage
   cheese
1 clove garlic, put through
   a press
1 teaspoon caraway seeds
1 teaspoon dill seeds
2 tablespoons chopped
   fresh herbs, such as
   basil, parsley, dill,
   fennel, marjoram,
   chives, thyme
2 tablespoons lemon juice
Freshly ground black
   pepper, to taste

1. Peel cucumbers if waxy and cut in half lengthwise. Scoop out seeds and cut in 3-inch long pieces.
2. Mix together cottage cheese, garlic, herbs, lemon juice, and pepper. Fill cucumbers, mounding mixture high.
3. Serve as hors d'oeuvres, a salad, or a light luncheon dish.

Note: This mixture is also nice on wide strips of green or red pepper.

MARINATED VEGETABLES VINAIGRETTE

Serves 8 to 10

1. Mix together all the ingredients for the marinade except oils and shallot and blend well.
2. Blend in oils and stir in shallot. Toss with prepared vegetables and marinate in refrigerator at least 1 hour, tossing occasionally.
3. Line a platter or individual plates with lettuce leaves and top with vegetables. Garnish with olives, radishes, and chopped fresh herbs.

For the vinaigrette:
Juice of 1 large lemon
½ cup red wine vinegar
2 cloves garlic, mashed to a purée or put through a press
2 teaspoons Dijon mustard
2 sprigs thyme, minced
1 teaspoon minced fresh basil
1 teaspoon minced fresh parsley
½ teaspoon tarragon
Sea salt and freshly ground black pepper, to taste
¾ cup safflower or vegetable oil
¾ cup olive oil
1 small shallot, minced

For the vegetables:
1 green pepper, cut in rounds, seeds and membranes removed
1 red pepper, cut in rounds, seeds and membranes removed
1 small or ½ large cucumber, scored down the sides with a fork and sliced
½ pound mushrooms, cleaned and trimmed
½ pound new potatoes, steamed until crisp-tender and sliced
½ pound tiny ripe tomatoes, left whole or cut in half
Lettuce leaves for the platter or plates
Olives, radishes, and fresh chopped herbs for garnish

MUSHROOMS FILLED WITH EGGPLANT PURÉE

Serves 4

1 tablespoon butter,
    safflower, or olive oil
1 clove garlic, minced or
    put through a press
12 to 16 large mushrooms,
    stems removed, wiped
    clean
¼ teaspoon thyme
Sea salt and freshly ground
    black pepper, to taste
1 recipe Eggplant Purée of
    your choice (pages
    32-33)
Thin strips of lemon peel
    for garnish (optional)

1. Heat butter or oil in a large, heavy-bottomed frying pan and add garlic and mushrooms. Sauté about 3 minutes, add thyme, salt and pepper, sauté another 2 minutes, and remove from heat.
2. Fill with Eggplant Purée of your choice, stuffing cavities as full as you can and mounding purée above the surfaces of the mushroom caps.
3. Heat through in a warm oven or serve at room temperature. Garnish, if you wish, with thin strips of lemon peel.

GARLIC BROCCOLI STEMS

This is a much better idea than throwing away broccoli stems when your recipe only calls for the florets. It is one of my most popular hors d'oeuvres. People always want to know what they are. You can also add these to salads.

Serves 6

Stems from 1½ pound
    broccoli, peeled and
    sliced ¼-inch thick
½ teaspoon sea salt
1 tablespoon wine vinegar
1 clove garlic, minced or
    put through a press
2 tablespoons olive or
    safflower oil

1. Toss broccoli stems with salt in a jar and refrigerate several hours. Pour off whatever liquid accumulates and rinse.
2. Add vinegar, garlic, and oil and shake together well. Refrigerate for several hours. Place in a bowl and serve.

TAPENADE BARQUETTES

Serves 6

1. Make Tapenade and hard boil eggs.
2. Peel eggs and cut in half crosswise. Carefully remove yolks and mash with Tapenade.
3. Turn tomatoes upside-down to drain 15 minutes. Blanch zucchini 3 minutes. Refresh under cold water and carefully scoop out seeds.
4. Fill eggs, tomatoes, and zucchini with Tapenade mixture. Arrange on a platter, garnish with parsley and radishes, and serve.

1 recipe Tapenade (page 30)
6 eggs
3 medium-sized ripe tomatoes, cut in half
2 medium zucchini, cut in half lengthwise and then into 3-inch lengths
Chopped fresh parsley for garnish
Radishes for garnish

POACHED EGGS À LA PROVENÇALE

Serves 4

1. Preheat oven to 400°F.
2. Heat oil in a heavy-bottomed frying pan and add garlic and shallot. Sauté until golden over low heat and add tomatoes, thyme, and a little salt.
3. Simmer 20 minutes, stirring occasionally, and add basil and freshly ground pepper.
4. Meanwhile poach eggs 3 minutes.
5. Transfer tomato sauce to a wide, low baking dish and place eggs on top of mixture.
6. Sprinkle each egg with a little Parmesan, and place in oven about 3 minutes, or just until Parmesan melts. Serve at once.

1 tablespoon olive oil or butter
1 large clove garlic, chopped (or more, to taste)
1 shallot, chopped
2 pounds ripe tomatoes, chopped
¼ teaspoon thyme
Sea salt and freshly ground black pepper, to taste
2-3 teaspoons fresh chopped basil
4-8 eggs
½ cup grated Parmesan cheese

PROVENÇAL AÏOLI MONSTRE

This is one of those festive Provençal dishes one sees at special occasions. During the grape harvest at Domaine Tempier, one of my favorite vineyards in the South of France, this is often served to celebrate the end of the harvest. Aïoli is sometimes called ''Provençal butter''.

Serves a crowd

1 recipe Aïoli (Garlic Mayonnaise — page 145)

2-4 artichokes, trimmed, steamed until tender, then cut in quarters and chokes removed

1 pound potatoes, steamed until tender and sliced

2 zucchini, cut into spears

1 small cauliflower, broken into florets and briefly steamed

½ pound carrots, cut into spears

1 bunch radishes, trimmed

2 sweet potatoes, steamed until tender and sliced (optional)

Other vegetables in season, such as tomatoes, green beans, asparagus. (Steam green vegetables until crisp-tender.)

1. Prepare Aïoli and refrigerate until ready to serve.
2. This can be served rustically, with vegetables in separate bowls and Aïoli in a large bowl. Pass Aïoli and let everyone take a portion, then pass the vegetables.
3. Or you can make a large, decorative platter and place the Aïoli in the middle or in mounds interspersed among the vegetables. Serve as an hors d'oeuvre or pass around as part of the meal.

GUACAMOLE

Serves 4 to 6

1. Cut avocados in half and scoop out pulp. Mash in a bowl with a pestle or wooden spoon, fork, or potato masher.
2. Add tomato and continue to mash together.
3. Stir in lemon juice, garlic, onion, cumin, and salt. Adjust seasonings (you may want a little more lemon or garlic).
4. Transfer to an attractive serving bowl. Place lettuce leaves on individual plates and serve garnished with tomato slices. This can also serve as a dip.

Preferably the dark, gnarled-skinned variety, which are much richer and less watery than the thin-skinned kind.

2 large or 3 small ripe avocados*
1 ripe tomato, chopped
Juice of 1 lemon
1 small clove garlic, puréed or put through a press
2-3 tablespoons minced onion
¼ teaspoon ground cumin
Sea salt, to taste
Lettuce leaves, for serving
Sliced tomatoes, for garnish (optional)

3
SOUPS

SPLIT PEA SOUP WITH CROÛTONS

Serves 6

1-2 tablespoons safflower oil, as necessary
1 onion, chopped
2 cloves garlic, minced or put through a press
2 carrots, chopped
1 leek, white part only, cleaned and sliced
2 cups split peas, washed
6 cups water
1 bay leaf
Sea salt and freshly ground black pepper, to taste
2 tablespoons butter
6 slices whole wheat bread, cut in cubes
1 additional clove garlic, minced or put through a press

1. Heat safflower oil and sauté onion and garlic until onion is tender.
2. Add carrots and leeks, sauté a few more minutes, and add split peas, water, bay leaf, salt, and freshly ground pepper to taste.
3. Bring to a boil, reduce heat, cover and simmer 1 hour, or until peas are tender. Remove bay leaf.
4. Purée half the soup in a blender or through a food mill and return to pot. Adjust seasonings.
5. Heat butter in a pan and add garlic and bread cubes. Sauté until cubes are golden (this can be done in advance). Remove from heat.
6. Heat soup through and serve, topping each bowl with a generous handful of croûtons. This freezes well.

EGG-LEMON SOUP

Serves 4 to 6

1. Bring vegetable stock to a boil, and add brown rice. Reduce heat, cover, and simmer 40 minutes, or until rice is cooked.
2. Beat eggs in a bowl and beat in lemon juice. Slowly stir in a ladleful of the soup, then transfer this mixture to the soup pot. Heat through but do not boil.
3. Adjust seasonings, adding salt and freshly ground pepper to taste. Serve, garnishing each bowl with a generous amount of chopped fresh parsley and a thin slice of lemon.

4 cups vegetable stock
½ cup raw brown rice, preferably long-grained
3 eggs
½ cup lemon juice
Sea salt and freshly ground black pepper, to taste
4 tablespoons chopped fresh parsley
Thin slices of lemon for garnish

WINTER TOMATO SOUP WITH VERMICELLI

Serves 4

1. Drain tomatoes and retain liquid. Return liquid to the can (or cans) and add enough water to fill. Put tomatoes through the medium disk of a food mill, or purée and put through a sieve.
2. Heat oil in a heavy-bottomed soup pot and sauté onion with 2 cloves of the garlic until onion is tender.
3. Add tomato purée and cook 10 minutes, stirring.
4. Add more garlic and the liquid from tomatoes. Add the tomato paste, salt and pepper to taste, and marjoram and thyme. Bring to a simmer and add vermicelli.
5. Cook until vermicelli is *al dente*. Taste again and add more garlic as desired. Serve.

2 pounds canned tomatoes
3-4 cloves garlic, to taste
1 tablespoon safflower or olive oil
1 onion, chopped
1 tablespoon tomato paste
Sea salt and freshly ground black pepper, to taste
¼ teaspoon thyme
½ teaspoon marjoram
4 ounces whole wheat vermicelli

LENTIL AND SORREL SOUP

Serves 4

1 tablespoon safflower oil
½ onion, chopped
2 cloves garlic, minced
1 cup lentils, washed
1 quart water
1 bay leaf
Sea salt and freshly ground
   black pepper
¼ pound sorrel, chopped
   fine
4 tablespoons milk or cream

1. Heat oil in a heavy-bottomed soup pot and add onion and garlic. Sauté until onion is tender and add lentils, water, and bay leaf. Bring to a boil, reduce heat, cover and cook 1 hour, or until lentils are tender. Add salt and freshly ground pepper to taste and remove bay leaf.
2. Purée lentils in a blender or through a food mill. Return to pot and bring to a simmer.
3. Add sorrel and cook 5 to 10 minutes. Correct seasonings, adding more garlic, salt, and pepper if you wish.
4. Stir in milk or cream and serve.

CREAM OF BROCCOLI SOUP

Serves 6

1 tablespoon butter or
   safflower oil
1 small onion, chopped
2 cloves garlic, minced or
   put through a press
½ teaspoon paprika
2 pounds broccoli florets
1 medium potato, peeled
   and diced
3 cups water or vegetable
   stock
Sea salt, to taste
Freshly ground black
   pepper, to taste
3 tablespoons chopped
   fresh parsley
1 cup milk (more to taste)
¾ cup freshly grated
   Parmesan cheese

1. Set aside 6 broccoli florets and steam just until bright green. Refresh under cold water and hold.
2. Heat butter or oil in a heavy-bottomed soup pot and sauté onion and garlic until onion is tender.
3. Add paprika, stir together, then add broccoli, potato, water and salt to taste.
4. Bring to a boil, reduce heat and simmer 20 minutes, uncovered. Purée through a food mill or in a blender and return to pot.
5. Stir in milk and parsley, add lots of freshly ground pepper, heat through and adjust salt. Thin out, if you like, with more milk.
6. Serve, topping each bowl with freshly grated Parmesan and broccoli florets. This can be frozen.

TURKISH BORSCHT

Serves 6

1. Heat oil in a large heavy-bottomed soup pot and add onion and garlic. Sauté a couple of minutes and then add the other vegetables, dill seeds, salt and pepper. Cook, stirring another minute, then add water or stock. Bring to a boil, cover, reduce heat and cook 1 hour.
2. Remove 2 cups from pot and purée in a blender or put through a food mill. Return to soup pot. Correct seasonings.
3. Serve, topping each bowl with a spoonful of yogurt.

1 tablespoon safflower oil
2 medium onions, chopped
3 cloves garlic, chopped
1 pound raw beets, chopped
2 cups shredded cabbage
2 stalks celery, sliced
2 medium potatoes, diced
1 medium green or red pepper, chopped
2 quarts water or vegetable stock
½ pound tomatoes, chopped
Sea salt and freshly ground black pepper
½ teaspoon dill seeds, crushed
Juice of 1 lemon
3 tablespoons chopped fresh dill
1 cup plain low-fat yogurt

TARRAGON SOUP

Serves 4 to 6

6 cups water
3 leeks, white part only,
    cleaned and cut in large
    pieces
2 carrots, coarsely sliced
1 stalk celery, coarsely
    sliced
1 onion, quartered
3 small potatoes, scrubbed
    and quartered
4 cloves garlic, peeled
1 bay leaf
6 whole peppercorns
Sea salt to taste
Freshly ground black
    pepper to taste
2 tablespoons chopped
    fresh tarragon
3 tablespoons freshly
    grated Parmesan
2 eggs, beaten (optional)

1. Combine all the ingredients except tarragon, freshly ground pepper, Parmesan, and eggs in a large soup pot and bring to a boil. Reduce heat and simmer uncovered 30 minutes to an hour. Taste and adjust salt. Drain and discard vegetables. Return broth to soup pot.
2. Heat broth and add tarragon and Parmesan. Stir and add freshly ground pepper to taste. Serve at once.
3. For a richer soup, beat eggs in a bowl and spoon in some of the hot soup, to which you have added the tarragon and cheese. Pour this back into the soup pot, heat through but do not boil, and serve with garlic croûton slices (below), if liked.

GARLIC CROÛTON SLICES

Several slices French or
    wholegrain bread
Olive oil
1 large cut clove of garlic

1. If using a thin baguette, simply cut into thin rounds; for larger loaves cut your slices into narrow strips.
2. Preheat the oven to 350°F. Brush the bread lightly with olive oil and bake until crisp in the oven.
3. As soon as you remove the bread from the oven, rub both sides of each slice with with cut clove of garlic. Serve immediately.

CURRIED PUMPKIN SOUP

Serves 6 to 8

1. Steam chopped pumpkin 15 to 20 minutes, or until soft. Purée through a food mill.
2. Combine pumpkin, milk, honey, and butter in a heavy-bottomed saucepan or soup pot and bring to a simmer over low heat. Stir together well to blend. Add spices and salt, and simmer gently 15 minutes. Do not boil.
3. Slowly add orange juice and rind. Simmer, stirring often, another 10 minutes. Correct seasonings and serve, topping each bowl with whipped cream or yogurt and a sprinkling of chopped pecans or sunflower seeds.

2 pounds fresh pumpkin, peeled and diced
1 quart milk
4 tablespoons mild honey (more to taste)
2 tablespoons butter
½ teaspoon freshly grated nutmeg (or to taste)
½ teaspoon ground cinnamon
½ teaspoon ground mace
½-1 teaspoon curry powder
¼ teaspoon ground ginger
Sea salt to taste
½-1 cup orange juice
1-2 tablespoons orange rind
Whipped cream or plain yogurt for garnish
2 tablespoons sunflower seeds or chopped pecans

BLACK BEAN SOUP

Serves 6 to 8

1 tablespoon safflower oil
1 onion, chopped
4 cloves garlic, minced
1 stalk celery, with leaves,
    chopped
1 pound black beans,
    washed and soaked for
    several hours
6 cups water or vegetable
    stock
1 bay leaf
1 teaspoon summer savory
Pinch of thyme
Pinch of sage
½ teaspoon celery seed
Sea salt and freshly ground
    pepper
Juice of 1 lemon
2 tablespoons dry sherry
Croutons and lemon slices
    for garnish
Chopped fresh parsley for
    garnish
Yogurt or crème fraîche for
    garnish

1. Heat safflower oil in a soup pot or Dutch oven
    and sauté onion with 2 cloves of garlic and the
    celery until onion is tender.
2. Drain beans and add to pot, along with water or
    stock, bay leaf, summer savory, thyme, sage,
    and celery seed. Bring to a boil, reduce heat, and
    simmer 1 hour. Add remaining garlic and sea salt
    and simmer another hour, covered.
3. Remove bay leaf. Purée half the soup in a blender
    or through a food mill and return to pot. Correct
    seasoning and add freshly ground pepper to
    taste. Stir in lemon juice and sherry, heat
    through, and serve, garnishing with yogurt or
    crème fraîche, croutons, lemon slices, and
    parsley.

*Note: This can be frozen, and will keep a few days in
the refrigerator.*

CHILLED CRANBERRY SOUP WITH POMEGRANATE SEEDS

Serves 4 to 6

1. Combine cranberries, onion, vegetable stock, and curry powder and bring to a boil. Reduce heat, cover, and simmer 10 minutes.
2. Dissolve cornstarch in orange juice and add to soup, along with honey. Simmer another 10 minutes. Remove from heat, let cool a moment, and purée in a blender with yogurt. Strain and stir in cream, lemon juice, and wine.
3. Cover and chill several hours or overnight. The flavor will mature during this time, so don't be concerned if it tastes rather flat before you chill it.
4. Serve chilled soup, topping each bowl with a spoonful of yogurt, a slice of orange, and a spoonful of pomegranate seeds.

¾ pound cranberries
1 small onion, chopped
5 cups vegetable stock or water
1-2 teaspoons curry powder
½ cup orange juice
¼ cup mild honey
1 tablespoon cornstarch
½ cup plain low-fat yogurt
½ cup cream
1-2 tablespoons lemon juice (more to taste)
¼ to ½ cup red wine, to taste
Additional yogurt for garnish (optional)
½ orange, cut in thin slices
½ cup pomegranate seeds

COLD CHERRY-LEMON SOUP

Serves 6

2½ pounds sweet dark
  cherries, stemmed,
  washed, pitted
Juice and grated rind of 2
  lemons
5 cups water
4-5 tablespoons mild honey
½ cup semi-dry white wine
1 tablespoon Kirsch
1 cup plain yogurt

1. Set aside 24 cherries. Combine remaining cherries with lemon juice and rind, water, honey, and white wine in a saucepan and bring to a simmer. Simmer 15 to 20 minutes.
2. Drain cherries and retain liquid. Purée in a blender, using some of the liquid to moisten, or through a food mill. Return puréed cherries and their liquid to the pot, stir in Kirsch, and adjust lemon juice and honey.
3. Chill the soup several hours. Just before serving stir in yogurt. Serve, garnishing each bowl with 4 of the cherries you set aside.

PEACH-YOGURT SOUP

Serves 6

3 pounds ripe peaches
4 tablespoons mild honey
3 tablespoons lemon juice
5 cups plain yogurt
1 cup fresh orange juice
3 tablespoons peach brandy
  (optional)
½ teaspoon cinnamon
½ teaspoon freshly grated
  nutmeg
¼ teaspoon ground ginger
½ teaspoon ground
  cardamom
½ teaspoon vanilla
½ cup slivered almonds for
  garnish

1. Set aside 6 of the peaches. Remove pits from remaining peaches and purée in a blender or through a food mill, along with honey and lemon juice. Place in a large bowl and stir in yogurt, optional brandy, orange juice, spices, and vanilla. Slice peaches you set aside and add to soup.
2. Serve, or cover and chill before serving. Garnish each bowl with slivered almonds.

RICH GARLIC SOUP WITH WHITE WINE

Serves 6

1. Set aside one clove of garlic for later use. Crush remaining cloves with the flat side of a chef's knife.
2. Combine water or stock, garlic, and salt and bring to a boil. Reduce heat, cover, and simmer 1 hour. Meanwhile toast the rye bread, and beat egg yolks and wine together in a bowl.
3. Strain soup, and gradually stir half of it into the wine-and-egg-yolk mixture. Pour this mixture back into soup pot, add freshly ground pepper, and adjust salt.
4. Mince clove of garlic set aside, or put through a press, and add to soup along with parsley or basil. Heat through gently.
5. Place a piece of toasted rye bread in each bowl and sprinkle on some cheese. Ladle in hot soup and serve.

2 heads garlic, cloves separated, skins left on
4 cups water or vegetable stock
Sea salt, to taste
6 slices rye bread
3 egg yolks
½ cup dry white wine
Freshly ground black pepper
4 tablespoons chopped fresh parsley or basil
1 cup grated Cantal or Cheddar cheese

CREAMY LEEK SOUP

Serves 4

1. Heat butter in a heavy-bottomed soup pot and sauté leeks and garlic over medium-low heat about 10 minutes, or until tender and aromatic.
2. Add vegetable stock and bread, bring to a simmer, cover, and cook 15 minutes.
3. Purée in a blender and return to pot. Season to taste with salt and pepper, and add a pinch of cayenne. Stir in yogurt or cream and serve.

1 tablespoon butter
4 large leeks, white part only, cleaned and sliced
2 cloves garlic, minced or put through a press
3 cups vegetable stock
½ pound stale French whole wheat bread, crusts removed, and diced
Pinch of cayenne
Sea salt and freshly ground black pepper, to taste
½ cup plain yogurt or cream

CREAM OF MUSHROOM SOUP

Serves 6 to 8

2 pounds fresh
  mushrooms, cleaned
  and trimmed
3 cups water or vegetable
  stock
3 tablespoons butter
2 cloves garlic, minced or
  put through a press
½ teaspoon dried thyme
½ small onion, finely
  minced or grated
3 tablespoons whole wheat
  flour
1¾ cups milk
2-3 tablespoons dry sherry,
  to taste
Sea salt and freshly ground
  black pepper, to taste
Chopped fresh parsley and
  sliced mushrooms for
  garnish

1. Set aside 6 attractive mushrooms to be used as garnish. Cut remaining mushrooms in half if they are large, leave whole if small, and combine with stock or water in a large saucepan.
2. Bring to a boil, reduce heat, and simmer gently, uncovered, about 45 minutes, or until mushrooms are tender and broth aromatic. Drain, retain broth, and reserve for later use.
3. Purée mushrooms in a blender, using broth to moisten.
4. Melt butter in a heavy-bottomed saucepan. When it begins to bubble, add garlic, thyme, and onion and cook a few minutes over low heat. Do not brown. Add flour and stir together with a wooden spoon to make a roux.
5. Cook this a few minutes, stirring, then slowly add 1¾ cups mushroom broth, stirring all the while with a wire whisk. Continue to stir until you have a smooth sauce. Pour back into soup pot, whisk in remaining broth, and simmer very gently 10 to 15 minutes.
6. Heat milk and stir in along with sherry. Season with salt, freshly ground pepper, and some of the parsley. Stir in puréed mushrooms, heat through but do not boil, and adjust seasonings.
7. Slice mushrooms, set aside and serve soup, garnishing with mushrooms and parsley. This can be frozen.

ZUCCHINI SOUP WITH DILL

Serves 4

1. Steam zucchini 10 minutes. Meanwhile sauté onion and garlic in oil until onion is tender.
2. Remove zucchini from heat and refresh under cold water. Set aside 12 rounds of zucchini and purée the rest, along with onion and garlic, in a food processor, through a food mill, or in a blender, using some of the vegetable stock to moisten.
3. Pour into a soup pot along with stock and stir together well. Reheat over medium heat and stir in dill and lemon juice. Season to taste with salt and freshly ground pepper.
4. Serve, garnishing each bowl with a dollop of yogurt or crème fraîche and three rounds of zucchini.

2 pounds zucchini, sliced ¼-inch thick
1 small onion, chopped
1 medium clove garlic, minced or put through a press
1 tablespoon safflower or vegetable oil
3 cups vegetable stock
3 tablespoons chopped fresh dill
Sea salt and freshly ground black pepper, to taste
Lemon juice, to taste
¼ cup plain yogurt or crème fraîche, for garnish

CHILLED SUMMER TOMATO-CUCUMBER SOUP

Serves 4

1. Combine all the ingredients except garnish in a blender and blend until smooth. Chill at least 1 hour. Serve garnished with herbs.

1 long cucumber, peeled and chopped
3 cups plain low-fat yogurt
1 clove garlic, chopped
1 teaspoon paprika
3 tablespoons tomato paste (or more, to taste)
Pinch of cayenne
Sea salt, to taste
2 tablespoons fresh chervil leaves or dill, for garnish

MINESTRONE

1 cup dried white beans,
soaked overnight in 3
times their volume
water
2 tablespoons olive oil
5 cloves garlic, minced or
put through a press
1 large onion, minced
2 leeks, white part only,
cleaned and sliced
2 carrots, sliced
½ small cabbage, shredded
2 potatoes, scrubbed and
diced
1 pound tomatoes, sliced
1 small can tomato paste
6 cups water or vegetable
stock
¼ teaspoon celery seed
3-inch rind of Parmesan
1 bay leaf
1 teaspoon oregano
½ teaspoon thyme
Sea salt and freshly ground
black pepper, to taste
1 teaspoon dried basil or 1
tablespoon fresh
1-2 zucchini, sliced thin
¾ cup fresh green beans,
trimmed and cut in half
1 cup (unshelled weight)
fresh or ¼ cup frozen
peas
4 ounces broken whole
wheat spaghetti
4 tablespoons chopped
fresh parsley
1 cup freshly grated
Parmesan cheese

This rich, luscious vegetable soup is even better served the day after it's made. The rind of Parmesan, which you can find at a cheese store (or cut it off the fresh Parmesan which you have bought for the soup) is the trick for a deeply aromatic broth.

Serves 6 to 8

1. Soak beans overnight or for several hours and drain.
2. Heat oil in a large, heavy-bottomed soup pot and add garlic, onion, leeks, carrots, and cabbage. Sauté, stirring over medium heat, about 10 minutes.
3. Add beans, potatoes, tomatoes, tomato paste, water or stock, celery seed, Parmesan rind, bay leaf, oregano, thyme, and *dried* basil (fresh basil should be added at the end of the cooking).
4. Bring to a boil, reduce heat, cover, and simmer 2 hours, or until beans are tender. Remove Parmesan rind and bay leaf.
5. Add salt and freshly ground pepper to taste, zucchini, green beans, peas, and spaghetti and cook another 15 minutes. Adjust seasonings.
6. Stir in parsley and fresh chopped basil and serve, topping each bowl with a generous amount of freshly grated Parmesan. This freezes well.

GAZPACHO ANDALUZ

Serves 4

1. Soak bread slices in water 5 to 10 minutes, or until soft. Squeeze out water.
2. Blend together all the ingredients for soup base until smooth.
3. Adjust seasonings. Chill several hours. The soup must be ice cold.
4. Serve soup and garnish each bowl with a heaping spoonful of the garnishes of your choice.

For the soup base:
1 pound ripe tomatoes, peeled
2-4 cloves garlic, depending on size and to taste, peeled
2 tablespoons olive oil
1-2 tablespoons wine vinegar, to taste
Sea salt, to taste
Freshly ground black pepper
1 cup ice-cold water
2 thick slices stale French whole wheat bread, crusts removed
1 small scallion, chopped, or 1-2 tablespoons chopped Spanish onion (optional)
½-1 teaspoon paprika (optional)
½ teaspoon crushed cumin seed (optional)
2 tablespoons fresh basil leaves (optional)

For the garnish:
1 small cucumber, peeled and finely diced
1 red or green pepper, seeds and membranes removed, finely diced
2 tomatoes, peeled and finely diced
4 tablespoons finely chopped onion
1 or 2 hard-boiled eggs, diced
½ cup diced croûtons

4

MAIN COURSES

QUICHE AUX FINES HERBES

For the crust:
1 cup whole wheat flour
½ teaspoon sea salt
4 ounces unsalted butter
*1-3 tablespoons ice cold
    water*

For the quiche:
1 tablespoon safflower oil
1 onion, chopped
*½ heaping cup fines herbes
    (parsley, chives, basil,
    chervil, tarragon,
    thyme)*
4 eggs, beaten
¾ cup milk
*2 tablespoons powdered
    milk*
*4 ounces Gruyère cheese,
    grated*
1 ounce Parmesan, grated
*Sea salt and freshly ground
    pepper*

1. Make crust. Mix together flour and salt and cut in
   butter. Add water as needed, gather into a ball,
   wrap in plastic wrap, and refrigerate 1 to 2 hours
   or, even better, overnight.
2. Preheat oven to 350°F. Roll out pie crust and line
   a buttered 10-inch quiche or pie pan. Bake the
   weighted crust 5 minutes and remove from oven.
3. Heat safflower oil in a frying pan and sauté onion
   until tender. Remove from heat and stir into
   beaten eggs, along with herbs. Mix together
   fresh and powdered milk and stir into egg
   mixture. Add cheeses and salt and pepper to
   taste.
4. Pour this mixture into prebaked pie crust and
   place in preheated oven. Bake 35 to 40 minutes,
   or until set and beginning to brown on the top.
   Remove from heat and serve.

*Note: This can also be served at room temperature
and freezes well.*

ZUCCHINI GRATIN

Serves 4 to 6

1. Preheat oven to 400°F.
2. Cut zucchini in half and scoop out seeds. Chop and steam 10 minutes, or until soft.
3. Remove from heat and mash with the back of a spoon or purée through a food mill. Add butter and milk and salt and pepper to taste. Stir in marjoram and parsley.
4. Butter a shallow baking or gratin dish and spread zucchini evenly over the bottom. Sprinkle with cheese, and if you wish, dot with a little butter.
5. Bake in the preheated oven 15 minutes, or until cheese is lightly browned.

3 pounds zucchini
2 tablespoons unsalted butter
1 tablespoon milk
Sea salt and freshly ground black pepper
2 tablespoons chopped fresh marjoram
3 tablespoons chopped fresh parsley
¾ cup grated Gruyère cheese
Additional butter (optional)

BROWN RICE AND BASIL GRATIN

Serves 6

1. Preheat oven to 350°F. Butter a 2-quart baking dish.
2. Heat oil or butter in a frying pan and add onion, garlic, and pine nuts or sunflower seeds. Sauté until onion is tender.
3. Add rice and basil, mix together well, and remove from heat. Add sea salt and freshly ground pepper to taste and stir in cheese.
4. Transfer to baking dish. Top with breadcrumbs and bake 30 minutes.

Note: This can also be used as a stuffing for vegetables. In this case stir in the cheese, then fill the vegetables, sprinkle on the breadcrumbs, and bake as directed above. The dish can also be frozen.

1 cup raw brown rice, cooked
1 tablespoon butter or safflower oil
½ onion, chopped
1 clove garlic, minced
2 tablespoons pine nuts or sunflower seeds
½ cup basil leaves, chopped
1 cup freshly grated Parmesan or Gruyère cheese
Sea salt and freshly ground black pepper
2 tablespoons whole wheat breadcrumbs

BROWN RICE AND BASIL EGGAH

Serves 4 to 6

1 cup raw brown rice,
  cooked
1 tablespoon butter or
  safflower oil
½ onion, chopped
1 clove garlic, minced
2 tablespoons pine nuts or
  sunflower seeds
½ cup basil leaves, chopped
1 cup freshly grated
  Parmesan or Gruyère
  cheese
Sea salt and freshly ground
  black pepper
6 eggs
2 tablespoons butter or
  safflower oil

1. Follow the directions for Brown Rice and Basil Gratin (see page 55) through to Step 3.
2. Beat eggs in a bowl while you heat butter or oil in a wide frying pan or omelette pan. Stir rice mixture into the eggs.
3. Spread egg and rice mixture over the bottom of the pan. Cook over low heat, shaking the pan gently and lifting occasionally with a spatula so eggs will run underneath, until just about cooked through. This will take about 10 minutes, perhaps a bit longer.
4. Loosen bottom of omelette with a spatula and carefully slide out onto a large plate. Reverse pan over plate and turn omelette back into pan. Cook another 5 minutes or so, until it is brown on the bottom and cooked through. Remove from heat and serve cut into wedges.

Note: This can also be served cold. It makes good picnic fare.

BAKED ZITI WITH TOMATO-BASIL SAUCE AND CHEESE

Serves 6 to 8

1. Make Tomato Sauce.
2. Preheat oven to 375°F.
3. Bring a large pot of water to a rolling boil, add salt, and cook pasta *al dente*. Drain and toss with a tablespoon of butter and half the Parmesan.
4. Oil a 3-quart baking dish or casserole and spread a third of the ziti over the bottom. Top with a third of the Ricotta, a third of the sauce and a third of the remaining Parmesan. Repeat the layers, ending with the Parmesan. Sprinkle breadcrumbs over the top and dot with remaining butter.
5. Bake 25 to 35 minutes in preheated oven, until bubbling. Remove from heat, let stand 5 minutes, and serve.

1 batch Tomato Sauce with Basil (page 131)
Sea salt for pasta water
1 pound ziti (tubular pasta)
1 tablespoon unsalted butter
1 cup freshly grated Parmesan
1½ cups Ricotta cheese
4 tablespoons breadcrumbs
1 additional tablespoon butter
Sea salt for pasta water

COUCOU À L'IRANIEN

A "Coucou" is an Iranian omelette, which is made like a Spanish omelette, flat. It is packed with herbs, and the nuts give it an interesting crunchy texture. I learned it from my French friend Christine, who learned it from her Iranian architect.

Serves 6

2 large bunches parsley,
   coarsely chopped, or 1
   bunch parsley, 1 bunch
   chervil
1-2 bunches mint, to taste,
   coarsely chopped
½ teaspoon saffron
12 eggs, beaten
Sea salt and freshly ground
   black pepper
12 walnuts, shelled and
   coarsely chopped
12 almonds, coarsely
   chopped
1 tablespoon olive oil
1 tablespoon vegetable or
   peanut oil

1. Combine herbs, saffron, eggs, sea salt, pepper, and nuts in a bowl and let sit 30 minutes.
2. Heat olive and vegetable oils together in a wide omelette pan or frying pan and add egg mixture. Cover with a large plate and let cook over low heat 10 minutes, or until almost cooked through.
3. Heat the broiler and finish omelette under the broiler, until it is browned on top and puffed. Can be served hot or at room temperature, cut into wedges. Serve with a green salad.

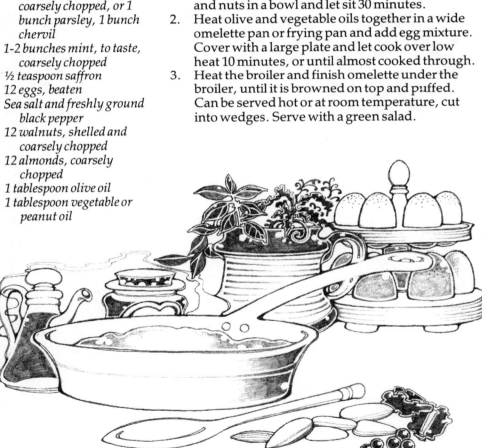

CHEESE, BREAD, AND TOMATO CASSEROLE

Serves 6 to 8

1. Preheat oven to 350°F. Butter a 2-quart baking dish or soufflé dish.
2. Layer bread, cheese, and tomatoes in that order, two layers of each in prepared baking dish.
3. Beat together eggs, milk, wine, thyme, mustard, pepper, and salt. Pour over cheese, bread, and tomatoes.
4. Bake 35 to 45 minutes, or until puffed and browned.

4-6 slices whole wheat bread
8 ounces Cheddar cheese, grated
3 ripe tomatoes, sliced
4 eggs
2 cups milk
2 tablespoons dry white wine
½ teaspoon thyme, dried or fresh
½ teaspoon dry mustard
Lots of freshly ground black pepper
Sea salt to taste

SORREL OMELETTE

Makes 1 omelette

1 bunch, or about ¼ pound
  sorrel
2 tablespoons butter
Sea salt and freshly ground
  black pepper
2 tablespoons plain yogurt
2 eggs
1 teaspoon milk

1. Wash and stem sorrel. Heat one tablespoon of butter in a frying pan or in your omelette pan and sauté sorrel until it wilts. This should only take a minute or two. The sorrel will lose its bright green color. Add salt and freshly ground pepper to taste, remove from heat, and stir in yogurt.

2. Heat remaining butter in omelette pan and meanwhile beat eggs together with milk and a little salt and freshly ground pepper.

3. When butter stops sizzling pour in eggs. Keep shaking and tilting pan with one hand as you gently lift the edges of the omelette with a spatula with the other hand, so that eggs on top can run underneath.

4. As soon as bottom of omelette is solid, spread sorrel down the middle. Turn omelette and cook for another half a minute or so, or until eggs are no longer runny; turn out onto a plate and serve.

SPINACH GNOCCHI WITH SAGE BUTTER

Serves 6

1. If you use fresh spinach, wash and stem, blanch and squeeze out excess water. Chop fine. Allow frozen spinach to thaw and squeeze out excess water. Chop fine.
2. Heat first 2 tablespoons butter in a saucepan over very low heat and add spinach, Ricotta, sea salt, and pepper to taste, and a little nutmeg. Using a wooden spoon, stir and mix together well, and cook 5 minutes. Remove from heat and stir in beaten eggs, 3 tablespoons flour, and 5 tablespoons of the Parmesan. Refrigerate at least 2 hours, or until stiff enough to handle.
3. Place additional flour on a plate. Take up the spinach-Ricotta mixture by heaping teaspoons (you can make them larger than this if you like) and roll them in flour, forming little balls coated with flour.
4. Bring water to a boil in a large pot. Add a heaping tablespoon salt, then drop in gnocchi one by one. When they float to the surface wait 3 to 4 minutes, then remove with a slotted spoon and set aside.
5. Melt remaining 4 tablespoons butter in a wide frying pan and add sage. Sauté about 2 minutes, then add gnocchi. Heat through, tossing gently with a wooden spoon to coat thoroughly with butter, and transfer to a warm serving dish. Sprinkle with remaining Parmesan and serve.

1½ pounds fresh spinach or 2 10-ounce packages frozen
2 tablespoons butter
1 cup Ricotta cheese
Sea salt and freshly ground black pepper
Pinch of nutmeg
2 eggs, beaten
3 tablespoons unbleached flour
½ cup freshly grated Parmesan
1-2 additional tablespoons unbleached white flour
4½ quarts water
4 tablespoons unsalted butter
10 leaves fresh sage, sliced

CAULIFLOWER GRATIN WITH GOAT CHEESE SAUCE

This dish can be assembled several hours in advance and popped into the oven 10 to 15 minutes before serving.

Serves 6

1 large cauliflower or two
   small ones, broken into
   florets
3 tablespoons olive oil or
   safflower oil
1 cup goat cheese, as soft
   and salt-free as you can
   find
½ cup low-fat milk or plain
   yogurt
1 clove garlic
¼ teaspoon thyme
Freshly ground black
   pepper, to taste

1. Preheat oven to 450°F
2. Steam cauliflower for 10 minutes, drain, and toss with 2 tablespoons of the oil in an oiled gratin dish.
3. In a food processor fitted with the steel blade, or in a bowl using a wooden spoon, or in a mixer, mash goat cheese and mix with garlic, milk or yogurt, thyme, and freshly ground pepper. Spread over cauliflower. At this point the dish can be set aside.
4. Just before baking, drizzle with 1 tablespoon oil. Place in oven and bake for 10 to 15 minutes, or until dish is sizzling. Serve at once.

FETTUCCINE WITH PESTO

Serves 6

Sea salt
1 tablespoon olive oil
1 pound whole wheat or
   spinach fettuccine
2 tablespoons hot water
   from the pasta
1 batch Pesto (page 138)
2 tablespoons butter
2 tablespoons roasted pine
   nuts, for garnish

1. Bring a large pot of water to a rolling boil, add a generous amount of salt, and a spoonful of oil. Add pasta and cook until *al dente*.
2. Add 2 tablespoons of cooking water to pesto, drain pasta, and transfer to a warm serving dish.
3. Toss with butter and serve, topping each serving with a generous helping of pesto and a sprinkling of pine nuts.

EGGPLANT PARMESAN

This dish involves a few steps but is well worth the time and effort.

Serves 6 to 8

1. Slice eggplant ½-inch thick. Arrange on plates and salt lightly. Weight with plates and let sit about 1 hour. Rinse and pat dry.
2. Meanwhile make a tomato sauce. Heat the tablespoon of olive oil in a heavy-bottomed saucepan and sauté onion and garlic over medium-low heat until onion is tender.
3. Add tomatoes and tomato paste, bring to a simmer, and simmer 30 minutes.
4. Add herbs, pepper, and cinnamon and simmer for another 15 minutes or so. Adjust seasonings.
5. Heat enough oil in a frying pan to coat the bottom. Dip eggplant slices in beaten egg and fry on both sides until crisp and browned. Drain on paper towels.
6. Preheat oven to 350°F.
7. Oil a large baking dish or casserole. Spoon in a very thin layer of tomato sauce and top with sautéed eggplant slices. Top with Mozzarella slices, then a layer of tomato sauce, then a layer of Parmesan. Make one or two more layers in this order, ending with Parmesan.
8. Bake in preheated oven 40 minutes. Remove from heat, sprinkle on parsley, and serve.

2 pounds eggplant
Sea salt
1 tablespoon olive oil
1 onion, chopped
2-3 cloves garlic, to taste, minced or put through a press
3 pounds tomatoes, chopped
2 tablespoons tomato paste
1 tablespoon chopped fresh basil or 1 teaspoon dried basil
½ teaspoon thyme (or more, to taste)
Freshly ground black pepper, to taste
Pinch of cinnamon
2 eggs, beaten in a bowl
Olive oil for frying
1 pound Mozzarella cheese, sliced thinly
1 cup grated Parmesan cheese
Fresh chopped parsley

BROWN RICE RISOTTO WITH BROCCOLI

Serves 6

*3 cups vegetable stock or
more if needed*
*½ teaspoon Vegex or
Marmite*
1 tablespoon safflower oil
¼ onion, minced
*1 clove garlic, minced or
put through a press*
1 cup brown rice, washed
½ cup dry white wine
½ pound broccoli florets
*¼-½ teaspoon thyme, to
taste*
*2 ounces freshly grated
Parmesan cheese*
*Sea salt and freshly ground
black pepper, to taste*
*1 egg, beaten with 4
tablespoons hot broth
(optional)*

1. Have vegetable stock simmering in a saucepan. Stir in *Vegex* or *Marmite*.
2. Heat safflower oil in a large, heavy-bottomed saucepan and sauté onion and garlic 3 minutes over medium heat.
3. Add rice and continue to sauté, stirring, until thoroughly coated with oil (another 2 to 3 minutes).
4. Add white wine and cook, stirring, over medium heat, until wine is just about absorbed. Pour in simmering stock, bring to a boil, reduce heat, cover, and simmer 30 minutes.
5. Add broccoli and thyme and more liquid if necessary, cover, and cook another 5 to 10 minutes. There should still be some broth.
6. Stir in Parmesan, add salt and freshly ground pepper to taste, and the optional egg beaten with stock; remove from heat and serve.

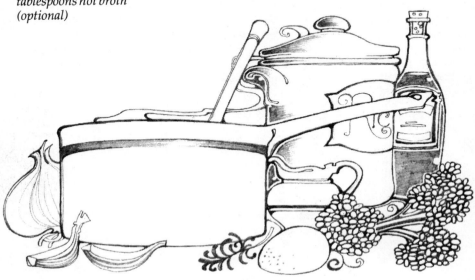

BROWN RICE RISOTTO WITH MUSHROOMS

Serves 6

1. Combine *Vegex* or *Marmite* and stock and bring to a simmer in a saucepan.
2. In another heavy-bottomed saucepan or casserole heat butter or oil and sauté shallots and garlic 3 minutes.
3. Add mushrooms and sauté another 3 minutes.
4. Add rice and continue to sauté, stirring over medium heat, until rice is thoroughly coated with oil or butter, another 2 to 3 minutes.
5. Add thyme and white wine and continue stirring over medium heat until wine is just about absorbed.
6. Stir in simmering stock, bring to a boil, reduce heat, and cover. Simmer 30 minutes and check to see if there is still enough broth. Add a little more if necessary.
7. Cover and cook another 5 to 10 minutes, or until rice is *al dente*. There should still be some broth.
8. Add parsley, Parmesan, salt and pepper to taste, and the optional egg. Mix together well and serve.

½ teaspoon Vegex *or* Marmite
3 cups vegetable stock or more if needed
2 tablespoons butter, safflower oil or olive oil, or a combination
2 shallots, minced
2 cloves garlic, minced or put through a press
½ pound mushrooms, cleaned, trimmed, and sliced fairly thin
1 cup raw brown rice, washed
½ cup dry white wine
½ teaspoon thyme
2 tablespoons chopped fresh parsley
½ cup freshly grated Parmesan cheese
Sea salt and freshly ground black pepper, to taste
1 egg, beaten with 4 tablespoons hot broth (optional)

LASAGNE

Serves 6 to 8

4 cups Rich Tomato Sauce
   (page 136)
12 to 15 sheets lasagne,
   either spinach or whole
   wheat
2 cups Ricotta cheese
2 eggs, beaten
2 small shallots, minced
1 clove garlic, puréed or
   put through a press
Freshly grated nutmeg
Freshly ground black
   pepper, to taste
1 pound Mozzarella cheese,
   sliced
1¼ cups freshly grated
   Parmesan cheese
¼ cup whole wheat
   breadcrumbs
Fresh chopped parsley, for
   garnish

1. First make Tomato Sauce, and set aside (can be done a day or two in advance).
2. Bring a large pot of water to a boil, add salt and a little oil and lasagne. Cook until *al dente*, drain, and rinse in cold water. Toss with a little olive oil and set aside.
3. Preheat oven to 375°F. Oil a large wide gratin or baking dish.
4. Sauté shallots and garlic in 1 tablespoon oil until tender — about 2 minutes.
5. Mix together Ricotta cheese, eggs, shallots, garlic, nutmeg to taste, and freshly ground pepper.
6. Spoon a thin layer of Tomato Sauce over bottom of baking dish. Over this lay three to four sheets of lasagne. Top with a third of the Ricotta mixture, then a third of the sliced Mozzarella, a third of the Tomato Sauce, a third of the Parmesan, and a third of the breadcrumbs. Repeat layers — noodles, Ricotta, Mozzarella, Tomato Sauce, Parmesan, and breadcrumbs — twice more.
7. Dot top layer of breadcrumbs with butter, if you wish, and bake in preheated oven 30 minutes, or until bubbling.
8. Remove from heat, let sit a few minutes, and serve, garnished with fresh chopped parsley.

SPINACH TIMBALE

Serves 6 to 8

1. Preheat oven to 325°F. Butter a soufflé dish and dust with a quarter of the breadcrumbs.
2. Wash spinach and, while still wet, wilt in a dry frying pan. Rinse under cold water and squeeze dry in a towel. Chop fine.
3. Heat butter or oil in a large frying pan and add onion and garlic.
4. When onion is tender, add spinach and sauté a few more minutes, or until spinach is coated with butter or oil. Remove from heat and place in a bowl.
5. Toss with remaining breadcrumbs, cheeses, and salt and pepper to taste.
6. Beat eggs in a bowl. Heat milk in a saucepan until it begins to tremble.
7. Remove from heat and whisk into eggs. Stir into spinach mixture and add a little nutmeg.
8. Pour this into soufflé dish and place in a pan of water. Bake in preheated oven 40 to 50 minutes, or until solid.
9. Remove from heat, let sit 10 to 15 minutes, and carefully unmold onto a serving plate. This can be frozen.

½ cup whole wheat breadcrumbs
2 pounds fresh spinach, washed, stems removed
1 tablespoon butter or safflower oil
½ onion, finely chopped
1 clove garlic, minced or put through a press
¾ cup grated Gruyère cheese
½ cup grated Parmesan cheese
Sea salt and freshly ground black pepper, to taste
4 eggs, beaten
1 cup milk
Pinch of nutmeg

PASTA WITH SPICY BROCCOLI

Serves 6

2 pounds broccoli, broken
  into florets
1 tablespoon olive oil
2 large cloves garlic,
  minced
1 small hot dried pepper,
  minced
1½ pounds tomatoes,
  sliced
2 tablespoons pine nuts,
  toasted
Sea salt, to taste
1 tablespoon vegetable oil
1 pound whole wheat
  spiral-shaped pasta or
  macaroni
¾ cup freshly grated
  Parmesan cheese
  (optional)

1. Steam broccoli florets 10 minutes and refresh under cold water. Begin heating water for pasta in a large pot.
2. In a wide, heavy-bottomed frying pan heat oil and sauté garlic and hot pepper about 1 minute, then add tomatoes and cook over medium-high heat 10 minutes.
3. Add toasted pine nuts and salt to taste, and stir in broccoli. Keep over a low flame while you cook pasta.
4. When water comes to a rolling boil, add salt a tablespoon of oil, and pasta.
5. Cook al dente, drain and toss immediately in a warm serving dish with tomato-broccoli sauce. Serve, and pass Parmesan in a separate bowl.

BAKED MACARONI WITH TOMATOES AND CHEESE

Serves 6

1. Mix together grated cheeses and toss with ground pepper.
2. Bring a large pot of water to a boil, add salt and a spoonful of oil, and cook pasta slightly less than *al dente*, as it will cook further in the oven. Drain and toss with olive oil.
3. Preheat oven to 375°F and butter a large, deep baking dish.
4. Spoon a third of the Tomato Sauce over bottom of baking dish and top with a third of the noodles, then a third of the cheese. Repeat layers and top with breadcrumbs. Dot with butter.
5. Bake, uncovered, 20 to 30 minutes, or until top browns and casserole is bubbling. Serve at once.

1 recipe Very Quick, Very Fresh Tomato Sauce (page 134)
½ pound Cheddar cheese, grated
1 cup freshly grated Parmesan cheese
Freshly ground black pepper
Sea salt
1 tablespoon oil
¾ pound elbow macaroni or flat noodles
2 tablespoons olive oil
⅓ cup whole wheat breadcrumbs
1 tablespoon butter

SPAGHETTI WITH FRESH PEAS AND HERB BUTTER

Serves 6

1 pound fresh peas in their
  pods, shelled
½ cup butter, softened
½ cup fresh chopped basil
½ cup fresh chopped
  parsley
1 clove garlic, puréed or
  put through a press
3 tablespoons fresh minced
  chives
Sea salt
1 pound very thin
  spaghetti (spaghettini
  or fusilli)

1. Bring a large pot of water to a boil.
2. Meanwhile steam peas 10 minutes, or until tender but still bright green, and drain.
3. Chop herbs and blend into butter along with garlic. Add a little salt if you wish.
4. When water comes to a rolling boil, add a generous amount of salt, a spoonful of oil, and pasta. Cook until *al dente*, drain, and toss immediately in a warm serving dish with peas and herb butter. Serve at once.

TORTILLA ESPAÑOLA

This is a flat omelette that can be served hot or cold.

Serves 4 to 6

1. Steam potatoes 10 minutes, until crisp-tender. Refresh under cold water and dry in a towel. Heat broiler.
2. In a 10-inch, well-seasoned or non-stick frying pan heat 1 tablespoon of oil and sauté onion and garlic until onion softens.
3. Add peppers and continue to sauté, stirring, about 5 minutes. Add potatoes and sauté another 5 minutes, or until they are soft.
4. Beat eggs in a bowl. Stir in salt and pepper to taste, and parsley or basil. Add a little more oil to pan and pour in eggs. Tilt pan so that eggs cover the surface evenly.
5. Let set while very gently shaking pan and lifting edges every now and again to let uncooked egg run underneath.
6. When omelette is just about cooked through place pan under broiler to finish, which should take about 3 minutes. It will puff up and brown a little. Serve hot or cool, cut in wedges.

½ pound new or boiling potatoes, scrubbed and diced small
2 tablespoons olive oil
1 small onion, chopped
1-2 cloves garlic, minced or put through a press
1 sweet green pepper, seeds and membranes removed, cut in strips
1 sweet red pepper, seeds and membranes removed, cut in strips
8 eggs, beaten
Sea salt and freshly ground black pepper, to taste
2 tablespoons chopped fresh parsley or basil

PROVENÇAL PIZZA

Serves 4 to 6

For the crust:
*2 cups whole wheat pastry
    flour*
½ teaspoon sea salt
1 teaspoon baking powder
½ teaspoon baking soda
½ cup water, as needed
2 tablespoons olive oil

For the topping:
*2 pounds tomatoes, seeded
    and chopped*
1 tablespoon olive oil
*1 large clove garlic, minced
    or put through a press
    (or more to taste)*
*½-1 teaspoon marjoram, to
    taste*
*¼-½ teaspoon thyme, to
    taste*
*½ cup grated Gruyère
    cheese*
*A handful of imported
    black olives*
¾ cup sliced mushrooms
2 tablespoons olive oil

1. Mix together flour, salt, baking powder, and baking soda. Add water and work in with your hands, then add olive oil and work in.
2. Oil a 10-inch pie pan or pizza pan with olive oil. Roll out crust ¼-inch thick and line pan.
3. Pinch a lip around the edge of the crust. Refrigerate until ready to assemble the pizza.
4. Heat 1 tablespoon olive oil in a heavy-bottomed frying pan or saucepan and sauté garlic 1 minute.
5. Add tomatoes and cook over a medium flame ½ hour, stirring occasionally.
6. Remove from heat and put through medium blade of a food mill. Season to taste with salt and pepper.
7. Preheat oven to 450°F. Spread tomato purée over pizza crust, then sprinkle with marjoram and thyme, grated Gruyère, olives, and mushrooms. Drizzle remaining oil all over.
8. Bake 15 minutes in preheated oven and serve. This freezes well.

PISSALADIÈRE (PROVENÇAL ONION PIZZA)

Serves 6

1. Heat oil in a large, heavy-bottomed saucepan and add onions, garlic, salt, and thyme.
2. Sauté over low heat, covered, 1½-2 hours, or until onions are reduced to a purée. Stir often. Add freshly ground pepper and adjust salt.
3. When onions are done, tilt casserole and press onions to one side so that juice runs to the other. Remove juice and set aside for crust.
4. Make pizza crust, substituting ¼ cup of juice for water in pizza crust recipe instructions. Roll out and line an oiled 10-inch quiche pan or pizza pan.
5. Preheat oven to 450°F.
6. Spread onion mixture over crust. Decorate with olives. Drizzle on a tablespoon of olive oil. Bake 15 minutes in preheated oven, or until crust is nicely browned. Serve hot.

2 tablespoons safflower or olive oil
2½ pounds finely chopped onions
2 large cloves garlic, chopped
½ teaspoon sea salt
1 teaspoon thyme
Freshly ground black pepper, to taste
1 pizza crust (page 72, but see instructions in Step 4)
16-20 black Niçoise olives
1 tablespoon olive oil

WHOLE WHEAT PIE CRUST

Enough for 1 large quiche or 2 smaller pies

⅔ cup butter
2 cups whole wheat pastry
    flour
½ teaspoon sea salt, unless
    using salted butter
Approx. 3 tablespoons ice-
    cold water

1. Combine flour and salt.
2. Cut butter into flour. Work between palms of hands until you have a mixture that resembles oatmeal or coarse cornmeal.
3. Add a tablespoon or two of water and gather up into a ball. If very crumbly add a little more water.
4. Wrap in plastic wrap and refrigerate 1 hour.
5. Soften with a rolling pin and roll out dough on a lightly floured work surface to a thickness of ¼ inch or less. Line a large quiche pan or two smaller pie pans. Refrigerate until ready to bake.
6. Before filling, weight by covering with a piece of foil and spreading dry beans over the surface. Prebake 5 minutes at 350°F.

MUSHROOM TART

This can be made in advance and reheated just before serving. It can also be frozen.

Serves 6 to 8

1. Make pie crust and line a 10-inch quiche pan. Chill until ready to use. Preheat oven to 350°F and prebake for 5 minutes. Set aside.
2. Brown onion in half the safflower oil. Set aside.
3. Heat butter and remaining oil in a large, heavy-bottomed frying pan and add mushrooms. Sauté, stirring, until mushrooms begin to soften and release liquid.
4. Add garlic, thyme, rosemary, salt, and a generous amount of pepper and sauté 2 to 3 minutes. Add the wine and continue to sauté until wine is absorbed.
5. Add soy sauce stir together. Stir in browned onions, and remove from heat.
6. Beat together eggs and milk. Toss together mushrooms and cheese.
7. Fill prebaked pie crust with mushroom mixture and pour in milk and egg mixture.
8. Bake in preheated oven 30 minutes, or until firm and browning on top. Remove from heat and serve, or cool and reheat just before serving.

1 Whole Wheat Pie Crust (opposite)
1 large onion, chopped
2 tablespoons safflower oil
1 tablespoon butter
1½ pounds mushrooms, large ones if possible, cleaned, trimmed, and cut in half if small or medium, or in quarters if large
1 large clove garlic, minced or put through a press
¼ teaspoon thyme, to taste
¼ teaspoon crushed rosemary, to taste
Sea salt and freshly ground black pepper, to taste
3 tablespoons dry white wine
1 teaspoon soy sauce
3 eggs
¾ cup low-fat milk
1 cup grated Gruyère cheese

CALZONES

Calzones are the Italian version of a turnover, a filling in a folded, sealed crust. You could fill them with any number of things. The one I've chosen here is a goat cheese filling seasoned with garlic and herbs.

Serves 8 to 10

For the crust:
1 tablespoon active dry
   yeast
1¼ cups lukewarm water
½ teaspoon honey
2 teaspoons sea salt
3 tablespoons olive oil
2 cups whole wheat flour
2 cups unbleached white
   flour, as needed

For the filling:
½ pound goat cheese
½ pound grated
   Mozzarella cheese
1 teaspoon crushed
   rosemary
1 teaspoon thyme
2 teaspoons chopped fresh
   sage (omit if not
   available)
Freshly ground black
   pepper
2 cloves garlic, minced or
   put through a press
3 tablespoons plain low-fat
   yogurt
1 egg, beaten

For the glaze:
4 tablespoons olive oil
2 cloves garlic, minced or
   put through a press

1. Dissolve yeast in water and add honey. Let sit for 10 minutes, or until it begins to bubble.
2. Stir in salt and oil. Add whole wheat flour and stir well. Add unbleached flour, ½ cup at a time, until you can turn out the dough.
3. Turn out dough onto a floured work surface and knead 10 minutes, adding more flour as necessary. Dough should be slightly sticky.
4. Oil bowl and place dough in it, seam side up first, then seam side down. Cover and place in a warm spot to rise for 1 to 1½ hours, or until doubled in bulk.
5. Meanwhile prepare filling. Sauté garlic gently in olive oil a minute or two.
6. Add to goat cheese in a bowl, and mash together with Mozzarella and herbs. Blend in yogurt and egg. Add freshly ground pepper to taste.
7. Preheat oven to 400°F.
8. Punch down dough and turn it out onto work surface, which you should dust with unbleached flour. Cut dough in half to facilitate rolling out.
9. Roll out to a thickness of ¼-inch. Using a small bowl as a guide, cut into circles about 6 inches in diameter.
10. Combine garlic and olive oil for glaze. Brush each circle with this mixture and top with 2 heaping tablespoons of the filling.
11. Fold dough over filling, pinch edges together tightly, then pinch and twist a lip around the

edge. Brush with garlic and olive oil mixture and place on an oiled baking sheet.

12. Bake in preheated oven 10 to 15 minutes, or until brown and crisp. Brush with oil halfway through baking and immediately upon removing from the oven. Serve at once. These freeze well.

ONION AND POTATO GRATIN

Serves 6

1. Preheat oven to 375°F. Butter a 1- to 2-quart gratin or baking dish.
2. Heat one tablespoon of oil in a large, heavy-bottomed frying pan and sauté onions with garlic over medium-low heat about 15 minutes, or until completely soft but not browned. Remove from heat.
3. Add the other tablespoon of oil, squeeze out all the moisture from grated potatoes, and add to pan. Sauté about 5 minutes, stirring. They should just begin to get soft.
4. Remove from heat and add to onions, along with thyme and parsley. Add a pinch of cayenne.
5. Beat together eggs and milk and stir into onion mixture with grated cheese. Add salt and freshly ground pepper to taste, and transfer to prepared baking dish.
6. Bake in preheated oven 40 minutes, or until top is browned. Serve at once. This can be frozen.

2 tablespoons safflower oil
1½ pounds onions, peeled and thinly sliced
2 cloves garlic, minced or put through a press
1 pound peeled and grated potatoes
½ teaspoon thyme
2 tablespoons chopped parsley
Pinch of cayenne
4 eggs
½ cup milk
¾ cup grated Gruyère cheese
Sea salt and freshly ground black pepper, to taste

GARLIC SOUFFLÉ

Despite its name this Garlic Soufflé does not reek of garlic. It is a rich cheese soufflé infused with garlic purée, which you obtain by baking the foil-wrapped garlic for a long time in the oven. It is a subtle masterpiece, one you won't soon forget and well worth the effort. This recipe is inspired by Alice Waters of Chez Panisse.

Serves 6 to 8

2 large heads garlic
2 tablespoons olive oil
1½ teaspoons thyme
Sea salt and freshly ground
    black pepper
1½ cups milk
1 onion, quartered
3 cloves unpeeled garlic
1 bay leaf
2 sprigs parsley
10 black peppercorns
¼ cup butter
¼ cup unbleached white
    flour
5 eggs, separated
1 cup grated Gruyère
    cheese
1 cup freshly grated
    Parmesan cheese
Pinch of cayenne
Butter for the soufflé dishes

1. Preheat oven to 325°F. Cut a large double-thickness square of aluminum foil and place whole heads of garlic on it. Drizzle olive oil over garlic and sprinkle with a little of the thyme, salt, and pepper.
2. Wrap in foil, sealing edges tightly but leaving some space around garlic. Place this foil envelope in oven and bake 1½ hours, or until garlic is very soft.
3. Remove from foil and allow to cool. Turn up oven to 450°F.
4. While garlic is baking combine milk, onion, 3 cloves of unpeeled garlic, bay leaf, some more of the thyme, the parsley, and peppercorns in the top part of a double boiler and simmer above boiling water (you can also do this in a pan over a heat diffuser) 1 hour.
5. Strain and measure out 1⅓ cups. If there is not enough because of evaporation, add a little plain milk. Return to pot and keep hot.
6. When garlic is cool enough to handle, squeeze out of skins and purée through a strainer. Stir into milk.
7. Heat butter in a heavy-bottomed saucepan and add flour. Stir together over low heat, and cook roux a few minutes, stirring all the while with a wooden spoon.
8. Remove from heat and whisk in hot milk all at once. Return to heat and cook, stirring with a whisk, until thick and smooth.

9. Let simmer in a double boiler or over a heat diffuser while you prepare eggs and cheese.
10. Combine the grated Gruyère with half the Parmesan. Separate eggs and beat egg whites until stiff.
11. Butter either 8 individual ramekins or a low, 2-inch gratin dish. Dust with half the remaining Parmesan.
12. Remove sauce from heat and stir in egg yolks, one at a time. Adjust salt, add a little cayenne and pepper, and fold mixture into beaten egg whites, along with cheese.
13. Carefully spoon this into prepared soufflé dishes, and sprinkle remaining Parmesan and thyme over tops.
14. Bake in hot oven 10 minutes, and serve immediately. It should be brown on top and creamy inside.

Note: If using a normal straight-sided soufflé dish, bake 20 minutes.

FETTUCCINE CON AGLIO E OLIO

Serves 6

1. Bring a large pot of water to a boil. Meanwhile heat olive oil with garlic in it in a small pan over very low heat. The garlic should simmer slowly and never brown.
2. When garlic is golden, remove from heat. This should coincide with water beginning to boil.
3. Add a tablespoon of salt to water, plus a tablespoon of cooking oil, and drop in pasta. Cook *al dente* and transfer to a warm serving dish with a slotted spoon or drain in a colander.
4. Toss at once with oil and garlic mixture, cheese, and parsley, and serve.

6 tablespoons olive oil
3 cloves garlic, finely minced
1 tablespoon sea salt
1 tablespoon oil
1 pound whole wheat or spinach fettuccine
¾ cup freshly grated Parmesan cheese
¾ cup fresh minced parsley

5

VEGAN MAIN COURSES

SPIRAL PASTA WITH RICH TOMATO SAUCE

Serves 4 to 6

1 tablespoon olive oil
1 onion, chopped
4 cloves garlic, minced
2 pounds ripe tomatoes,
    chopped
½ cup tomato paste
1 bay leaf
2 teaspoons oregano
1 tablespoon chopped fresh
    basil, or 1 teaspoon
    dried
Pinch of cinnamon
Sea salt and freshly ground
    black pepper
½ pound spiral-shaped
    pasta

1. Heat olive oil in a heavy-bottomed saucepan and add onion and 2 cloves of garlic. Sauté until onion is tender and add tomatoes, tomato paste, and bay leaf. Bring to a simmer, cover, and simmer 30 minutes.

2. Add remaining garlic, oregano, basil, cinnamon, and salt to tomato sauce. Continue to simmer, uncovered, another 30 minutes or even longer. Adjust seasonings and add freshly ground pepper to taste. If the sauce tastes a little bitter, add a teaspoon of honey.

3. Bring a large pot of water to a boil, add salt and a spoonful of cooking oil, and pasta. Cook until *al dente*, drain, and toss immediately with tomato sauce in a warm casserole. Serve at once.

Note: The sauce freezes well and will keep several days in the refrigerator.

RED BEAN GOULASH

Serves 6 to 8

1. Heat 1 tablespoon safflower oil in a large bean pot or soup pot and sauté onions with 2 cloves of garlic until onions begin to soften. Add carrots and celery and continue to sauté a few more minutes. Drain beans, rinse, and add to the pot, along with summer savory, oregano, tomatoes, water, and bay leaf. Bring to a boil, cover, and reduce heat. Simmer 2 hours, adding remaining 2 cloves of garlic and salt to taste halfway through the cooking.
2. Correct seasoning for beans, adding freshly ground pepper to taste, and more sea salt and garlic if you wish. Drain and retain liquid.
3. In a heavy-bottomed saucepan or frying pan, heat the additional 2 tablespoons of safflower oil and add additional onion and 2 cloves of garlic. Sauté over low heat until onion is soft. Add unbleached white flour and paprika and stir together with a wooden spoon. Cook this roux over low heat about 3 minutes, stirring.
4. Off the heat, whisk liquid from beans into roux. Return to heat and bring to a simmer, stirring. When mixture is thick, stir back into beans. Add parsley and vinegar, bring to a simmer, taste, and adjust seasonings.
5. Serve, topping, if you like, with chives.

Note: This makes a complete, filling meal if served with whole wheat noodles. Try to find wide ones, which will give the dish a more Hungarian nature. This can be frozen and will keep about 3 days in the refrigerator.

1 tablespoon safflower oil
2 onions, chopped
4 large cloves garlic, minced
2 carrots, sliced
2 stalks celery, chopped, with leaves
1 pound red beans, washed and soaked overnight
1 teaspoon summer savory
1 teaspoon oregano
1 ½ pounds tomatoes, peeled, chopped (may use canned)
2 quarts water
1 bay leaf
Sea salt and freshly ground black pepper
2 additional tablespoons safflower oil
1 additional small onion, minced
2-3 additional cloves garlic, minced
2 tablespoons unbleached white flour
2 tablespoons paprika
The liquid from the beans
½ cup minced parsley
2 tablespoons wine vinegar
Additional sea salt, pepper, and paprika to taste
Chives for garnish (optional)
½ pound wide whole wheat noodles (optional)

RICE WITH TOFU, POTATOES, AND CUMIN

Serves 6

3 cups water (more as
    needed)
2 tablespoons safflower oil
    (more as needed)
2 tablespoons whole cumin
    seeds
1 large or 2 small potatoes,
    scrubbed and diced
    small
4 ounces tofu, diced
1 ½ cups raw brown rice
¼ - ½ teaspoon sea salt, to
    taste
½ teaspoon turmeric

1. Have water simmering.
2. Heat oil in a heavy-bottomed saucepan and add cumin seeds. When they begin to pop, after about 15 seconds, add potatoes and tofu. Cook, stirring, until potatoes begin to brown. Add rice and a little more oil if pan is too dry, and cook, stirring, a couple of minutes.
3. Add water, salt, and turmeric, and bring to a boil. Reduce heat, cover, and simmer 35 minutes. Uncover, check liquid, and add a little more if pan is dry. Cook another 5 to 10 minutes, or until liquid is absorbed and rice is cooked through.

CURRIED MILLET WITH GARLIC

Serves 4

¾ cup millet
1 tablespoon safflower or
    peanut oil
½ teaspoon cumin seeds
1 small onion, chopped
2 cloves garlic, sliced thin
½-inch piece fresh ginger,
    minced or grated
½ teaspoon turmeric
1 ½ teaspoons curry
    powder
1 ½ cups water
Sea salt, to taste

1. Roast millet in a dry frying pan until it begins to smell toasted. Set aside.
2. Heat oil in a heavy-bottomed saucepan and add cumin seeds, onion, and garlic.
3. Sauté until onion is tender and add ginger, turmeric, and curry powder.
4. Sauté another minute and add millet. Stir together and pour in water.
5. Bring to a boil, add salt, reduce heat, cover, and simmer for 35 minutes. Check to see if water has been absorbed, and if it has, add 4 tablespoons boiling water and cook, undisturbed, another 10 minutes.
6. Remove from heat and let sit for 15 minutes, covered, before serving.

LENTILS AND BULGHUR WITH PARSLEY AND MINT

Serves 4

1. Heat 1 tablespoon of olive oil in a heavy-bottomed saucepan or Dutch oven and add half the onion and 2 cloves of garlic. Sauté 2 minutes, or until onion is soft.
2. Stir in lentils, water, and bay leaf and bring to a boil. Add salt, reduce heat, cover, and simmer 30 to 45 minutes, or until lentils are soft but not mushy. Adjust seasonings, add some pepper, and remove bay leaf.
3. Stir in bulghur, cover pot, and let sit 30 minutes to an hour off the heat. Stir once to make sure all the bulghur is being infused with the cooking liquid.
4. Heat remaining tablespoon of olive oil in a wide frying pan and add remaining onion and garlic. Sauté a minute or two and stir in cumin and coriander. Sauté another couple of minutes and stir in lentils and bulghur. Cook, stirring, a minute or two to heat through, and stir in parsley and mint. Adjust seasonings and serve.

2 tablespoons olive oil
1 onion, chopped
3 cloves garlic, minced
⅔ cup lentils, washed
2½ cups water
1 bay leaf
Sea salt and freshly ground
    black pepper to taste
⅔ cup bulghur
1 teaspoon ground cumin
1 teaspoon ground
    coriander seeds
3 tablespoons chopped
    fresh parsley
2 tablespoons chopped
    fresh mint

Note: This will keep up to three days in the refrigerator, and it makes a good stuffing for vegetables (see following recipe).

TOMATOES AND ZUCCHINI STUFFED WITH LENTILS AND BULGHUR

Serves 4 to 6

*1 recipe Lentils and
  Bulghur with Parsley
  and Mint (page 83)*
4-6 firm, ripe tomatoes
4-6 small zucchini
*Additional parsley and
  mint for garnish
  (optional)*

1. Cook lentils and bulghur as in the recipe on page 83, up to Step 4.
2. Preheat oven to 350°F.
3. Cut tops off tomatoes, about ½ inch down from stems, and scoop out seeds with a small spoon. Discard seeds and gently scoop or cut out some of the inner flesh. Chop flesh.
4. Cut zucchini in half lengthwise and steam 5 minutes in a covered pot. Remove from heat, refresh under cold water, and pat dry. Using a small spoon, carefully scoop out seeds and some of the inner flesh, leaving a ½ inch thick shell. Chop scooped out zucchini.
5. Now proceed with Step 4 of the Lentils and Bulghur recipe, but add diced tomato and zucchini pulp to the onions. When onion is tender, proceed as directed.
6. Carefully fill tomatoes and zucchini with lentil-bulghur mixture and place in an oiled baking dish. Heat through for 15 minutes in preheated oven and serve, topping if you wish with chopped fresh parsley and/or mint.

Note: This can be prepared a few hours in advance, up to the baking point.

BAKED BEANS WITH FRUIT

Serves 6 to 8

1. Soak beans in water overnight, or for at least several hours. Drain and combine with same quantity of water in a large saucepan. Bring to a boil, add 1 teaspoon sea salt, and cook about 1 to 1½ hours, until tender but not mushy. Drain, reserving 1 cup of liquid.
2. In a small bowl, dissolve mustard in bean liquid and combine with finely chopped onion and salt and pepper to taste. Stir this into beans, along with fresh and dried fruit.
3. Preheat oven to 325°F. Oil a 2-quart casserole or baking dish.
4. Pour bean mixture into prepared casserole. Combine honey and molasses and pour evenly over top.
5. Cover and bake 1 hour, then remove cover and bake another 30 minutes. Serve steaming hot, with Texas Cornbread (page 154).

1 pound dried white beans
or soybeans, washed
and picked over
1 quart water
1½ teaspoons sea salt
1½ teaspoons dry mustard
1 onion, chopped
2 apples, sliced
½ cup dried apricots
½ cup mild honey
4 tablespoons molasses

PUMPKIN STUFFED WITH MILLET AND FRUIT

This is a delightful substitute for turkey if you are doing a meatless Thanksgiving dinner. It also makes a fine side dish

Serves 8 to 10

2 cups raw millet
1 cup raisins
Sherry to cover the raisins
1 large pumpkin, about 14 inches in diameter
3 ounces vegan margarine, in all
¾ pound apples, peeled and sliced
¾ pound pears, peeled and sliced
¾ cup slivered almonds
½ cup dried apricots, chopped
4 tablespoons mild honey
½-1 teaspoon cinnamon
½ teaspoon nutmeg
½ teaspoon mace
½ teaspoon allspice
½ teaspoon cardamom
½ teaspoon freshly ground black pepper
Sea salt to taste
Fresh autumn-colored flowers, for garnish

1. Cook millet, and while doing so soak raisins in sherry to cover. Drain raisins after 30 minutes.
2. Preheat oven to 325°F.
3. Cut out top of pumpkin and remove all seeds and strings. Using a spoon, carefully scrape out a layer of the flesh from the inside of the pumpkin, being careful not to break through the outside. Remove about 1 lb and dice. Steam until tender, about 10 minutes, and set aside.
4. Heat 2 tablespoons of margarine in a large, heavy frying pan and sauté apples, pears, almonds, and apricots about 5 minutes. Add 2 tablespoons honey, spices, cooked millet, steamed pumpkin, and sea salt to taste, and cook together another few minutes, stirring. Correct seasonings. Remove from heat.
5. Melt remaining margarine and stir in remaining honey. Add a little cinnamon and brush inside of pumpkin with this. Spoon filling into pumpkin and replace lid. Place on an oiled baking sheet or in a large baking dish and bake 1 hour in preheated oven. Place on a large serving platter, surround with flowers, and serve.

EGGPLANT, POTATOES, GARLIC, AND TOFU STEWED IN BRANDY

The vegetables here are stewed very slowly for 2 hours and absorb the perfume of the brandy. The eggplant falls apart and thickens the combination. It is a heavenly dish. You may add more water if it seems dry to you.

Serves 6 to 8

1. In a large, heavy-bottomed, lidded casserole heat oil and brown onion over moderate heat.
2. Add tofu and soy sauce and sauté another 5 minutes. Add flour and stir together a minute or two, then add garlic and eggplant and a little more oil if necessary.
3. Sauté about 3 minutes to coat with oil. Add potatoes, brandy, water or stock, and *Vegex* or *Marmite* and bring to a simmer.
4. Reduce heat, place over very low heat, preferably on flameproof pad, cover, and simmer slowly 2 hours. Stir from time to time, and add more water or stock if necessary.
5. Add pepper, taste and add salt if you wish, and serve, garnishing with leaves of fresh thyme.

1 tablespoon safflower oil
1 onion, sliced
½ pound tofu, diced
1 tablespoon soy sauce
1 teaspoon whole wheat flour
Cloves from 1 head garlic, peeled and left whole
1 pound eggplant, diced
1 pound boiling potatoes, diced
½ cup brandy
½ cup water or vegetable stock
½ teaspoon Vegex *or* Marmite
Freshly ground black pepper, to taste
Fresh thyme for garnish

CURRIED ZUCCHINI

Serves 4 to 6

1 tablespoon safflower or
    peanut oil
1 small onion, sliced
1 clove garlic, minced or
    put through a press
½ teaspoon grated fresh
    ginger
2 teaspoons curry powder
    (or more, to taste)
½ teaspoon ground cumin
    or crushed cumin seeds
2 pounds zucchini, sliced
    diagonally ¼-inch thick
2 tablespoons water or
    vegetable stock
Sea salt and freshly ground
    black pepper, to taste
Fresh chopped mint or
    coriander, for garnish
Chutney or raisins, for
    garnish

1. Heat oil in a frying pan and sauté onion and garlic until onion begins to soften — about 3 minutes.
2. Add ginger, curry powder, and cumin and sauté another 3 minutes.
3. Add zucchini, stir together for a minute or two, and add water or vegetable stock.
4. Cook, stirring from time to time, 15 minutes. Add salt and pepper to taste and adjust seasonings.
5. Remove from heat.
6. Serve with grains, garnishing with chopped fresh mint or coriander and chutney or raisins.

SAUTÉED TOFU AND VEGETABLES

Serves 6 to 8

1. Combine all ingredients for tofu in a saucepan and simmer 10 minutes. Drain and retain marinade.
2. Mix together ingredients for sauce and set aside.
3. Heat a wok or a large frying pan over a high flame and add oil. Stir-fry garlic, ginger, and onion 2 minutes, or until onion is translucent.
4. Remove from pan, place in a bowl, and add to pan mushrooms and tofu. Stir-fry 3 minutes and add celery, walnuts, and snow peas. Stir-fry 1 more minute, or until peas are bright green.
5. Return other ingredients to wok and add bean sprouts. Toss together and pour in sauce. Cook, stirring, until sauce glazes vegetables.
6. If sauce doesn't thicken within a couple of minutes, add another teaspoon of cornstarch dissolved in a little water. Serve over grains or noodles.

For the tofu:
¾ pound tofu, diced
½ cup soy sauce
½ cup water
1 clove garlic, crushed
1 teaspoon minced or
 grated fresh ginger
½ teaspoon cinnamon
¼ teaspoon ground allspice
¼ teaspoon crushed anise
⅛ teaspoon ground cloves

For the sauce:
½ cup strained marinade
 from the tofu
1 cup vegetable stock
2 tablespoons dry sherry
1 teaspoon honey
1 teaspoon vinegar
1 tablespoon cornstarch
 (more, if necessary)

For the vegetables:
2 tablespoons safflower,
 peanut, or sesame oil
1 clove garlic, minced or
 put through a press
1 teaspoon minced or
 grated fresh ginger
1 onion, sliced thinly
1½ cups sliced fresh
 mushrooms
1 stalk celery, sliced
½ cup walnuts
1 cup trimmed snow peas
½ pound mung bean
 sprouts

CURRIED RICE WITH LENTILS AND GARLIC

Serves 6

1 tablespoon safflower oil or
   peanut oil
4 cloves garlic, sliced
1 small onion, chopped
½-inch piece of fresh
   ginger, minced or
   grated
½ teaspoon turmeric
½ teaspoon crushed cumin
   seeds
¼ teaspoon ground allspice
2 teaspoons curry powder
   (or more, to taste)
¾ cup raw brown rice,
   washed
1 cup lentils, washed and
   picked over
3 cups water
Sea salt, to taste
Plain soy yogurt and
   raisins for garnish

1. Heat oil in a large, heavy-bottomed, lidded saucepan and sauté garlic, onion, and ginger until golden. Add spices and sauté another few minutes.
2. Add rice and lentils and sauté a few minutes to coat with oil, then add water. Bring to a boil, add salt to taste, reduce heat, cover, and simmer 35 minutes.
3. Check for water, pour in another 4 tablespoons boiling water if all the water has been absorbed, cover, and simmer another 10 minutes.
4. Remove from heat, let sit 10 to 15 minutes, and serve topped with soy yogurt and raisins.

POLENTA WITH PAN-FRIED MUSHROOMS

Serves 6 to 8

1. Make Pan-Fried Mushrooms and set aside.
2. Bring water to a rolling boil in a large, heavy-bottomed soup pot or saucepan. Add salt and turn heat to medium-low so that water is just simmering.
3. Add cornmeal in a very slow stream, stirring all the while with a long-handled wooden spoon. You should be able to see the separate grains as you pour. One way to do this is to take up handfuls of the polenta and let it slip through your fingers.
4. Once all the polenta has been added, continue to stir steadily 15 to 20 minutes, or until mixture is stiff and tears away from sides of the pot as you stir.
5. If you want a creamier polenta, add an extra cupful of water and don't stir quite as long. When the polenta is cooked, transfer it to a large platter, make a shallow depression in the middle, and pour on the mushrooms. Serve at once.

*1 recipe Pan-Fried
  Mushrooms (page 109)*
*1 ½ cups coarse-grained
  cornmeal or packaged
  polenta*
1 ½-2 teaspoons sea salt
*6 cups water (or more for a
  creamier polenta)*

BARLEY WITH MUSHROOMS AND GARLIC

Serves 6

3 cups vegetable stock
1 tablespoon safflower oil,
    more as needed
1 onion, chopped
1 pound mushrooms,
    cleaned, stems trimmed
    and sliced
2-4 cloves garlic, minced
    (to taste)
1 tablespoon soy sauce
2 tablespoons dry white
    wine
½ teaspoon thyme
1 cup barley, washed
Sea salt and freshly ground
    black pepper, to taste

1. Bring stock to a boil in a saucepan.
2. Preheat oven to 350°F.
3. Heat oil in a large, lidded casserole and sauté onion until tender. Add mushrooms and garlic and sauté until mushrooms begin to release some of their liquid — about 2 to 3 minutes.
4. Add soy sauce, white wine, and thyme and continue to sauté another 3 minutes.
5. Stir in barley and sauté 1 minute, then pour in broth and bring to a second boil. Add a little salt and pepper, cover, and place in preheated oven.
6. Bake 30 to 40 minutes, or until barley is tender. Check liquid from time to time and add more if necessary.

SPICED BULGHUR PILAF WITH NUTS AND RAISINS

Serves 4 to 6

1. Heat oil in a heavy-bottomed saucepan or lidded frying pan or wok and sauté almonds until they begin to brown. Remove from oil and transfer to a bowl. Repeat the process with cashews and pine nuts.
2. Add raisins, and as soon as they puff up remove from heat.
3. Add cumin, onion, garlic, and ginger and sauté until onion is tender.
4. Add bulghur and stir together, then stir in nuts and raisins and water. Bring to a boil, add salt to taste, cover, reduce heat, and simmer 15 minutes, or until water is absorbed and bulghur tender.
5. Remove from heat and let sit 15 minutes. Serve garnished with raisins and sunflower seeds or pine nuts, and serve yogurt on the side.

1 cup bulghur
2 tablespoons safflower, peanut, or vegetable oil
2 tablespoons slivered almonds
2 tablespoons halved cashews
2 tablespoons pine nuts
5 tablespoons sultanas
½ teaspoon cumin seeds
½ teaspoon crushed cardamom seeds
1 small onion, sliced very thin
1 clove garlic, minced
1-inch piece fresh ginger, peeled and grated or minced
3 cups water
Sea salt, to taste
Additional raisins and pine nuts or sunflower seeds, for garnish

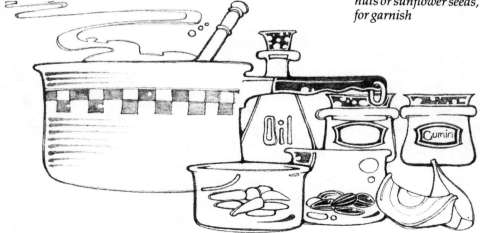

SLOW-COOKED BEANS AND RICE

This is one of the most exquisite bean dishes I know of, and it's so simple. The extremely slow cooking of the beans, with all the garlic, yields a rich, thick broth, and the beans are very soft and digestible.

Serves 6

1 pound red or black beans, washed and picked over
1 large onion, chopped
6 large cloves garlic, minced
8 cups water
Sea salt and freshly ground black pepper, to taste
¾ cup brown rice, cooked

1. Heat oven on its lowest setting.
2. Combine beans, onion, garlic, and water in a large, lidded, ovenproof casserole and place in oven. Do not add salt.
3. Cook in slow oven overnight, or all day, 6 to 10 hours.
4. Check liquid after 6 or 7 hours and add more if necessary.
5. When beans are tender and liquid is thick and soupy, add salt to taste, and stir in cooked brown rice and some pepper.

WHITE BEANS À LA PROVENÇALE

Serves 6

1. Soak beans in three times their volume water overnight or for several hours.
2. In a large, heavy-bottomed saucepan or casserole heat oil and sauté 1 onion and 2 cloves garlic until onion is tender.
3. Drain beans and add them, along with fresh water and bay leaf.
4. Bring to a boil, reduce heat, cover, and simmer 1 hour, or until tender. Add salt to taste. Remove bay leaf, drain, and retain cooking liquid.
5. Heat additional olive oil in a wide, heavy-bottomed frying pan or casserole and sauté extra garlic for 1 minute. Add tomatoes and herbs, salt to taste, and simmer 5 minutes.
6. Add beans, along with a cup of their cooking liquid, and continue to simmer, covered, 15 minutes. Adjust seasonings and serve.

1 pound beans, washed and picked over
1 tablespoon olive oil
1 onion, chopped
2 cloves garlic, minced or put through a press
5 cups water
1 bay leaf
Sea salt, to taste
1 additional tablespoon olive oil
1-2 additional cloves garlic, minced or put through a press
1 pound tomatoes, peeled and chopped
Fresh or dried thyme, to taste
Fresh or dried basil, to taste
Freshly ground black pepper, to taste

POTAJE DE GARBANZOS (TOMATO AND CHICKPEA STEW)

This is based on a Spanish dish that is served as a thick soup. Serve it that way or as a side or main dish. It is a meal in itself, with whole grain bread and a salad.

Serves 6

1 tablespoon olive oil
1 large onion, chopped
4 large cloves garlic, minced
1 teaspoon paprika (or more, to taste)
1 pound ripe tomatoes (fresh or canned), peeled, seeded, and chopped
1 bay leaf
4 tablespoons tomato paste
2 medium boiling potatoes, diced
1 teaspoon thyme
1 teaspoon oregano
2 cups broth from the beans
2 cups chickpeas, cooked (reserve the broth)
Sea salt and freshly ground black pepper, to taste

1. In a heavy-bottomed saucepan or casserole heat olive oil and add onion and garlic. Sauté until onion is tender, and add paprika.
2. Stir a minute, and add tomatoes, bay leaf, and tomato paste. Simmer together over medium heat 10 minutes.
3. Add potatoes, thyme, oregano, broth from beans, chickpeas, and salt to taste.
4. Bring to a boil, reduce heat, cover, and simmer 30 minutes, or until potatoes are tender. Stir from time to time. Add plenty of ground pepper and adjust seasonings. Serve.

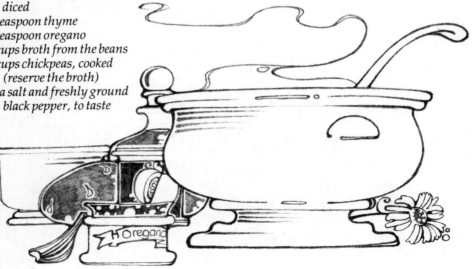

SUCCOTASH WITH TOMATOES AND GARLIC

Succotash is a Native American dish that is based on the combination of corn and beans. It has evolved into a dish that is usually made with lima beans though other beans could be substituted.

Serves 6 to 8

1. First cook beans. In a heavy-bottomed saucepan or bean pot heat safflower oil and sauté onion and the first 6-8 cloves of garlic until onion is tender.
2. Add beans and water, bring to a boil, cover, and reduce heat. Cook 1 to 2 hours, or until tender but not mushy. Add salt to taste.
3. Remove from heat, drain, and reserve liquid. Save what you don't use in the succotash for soups.
4. Heat olive oil in your bean pot and add remaining garlic and rosemary and thyme. Sauté a few minutes over low heat, or until garlic begins to turn gold.
5. Add red wine, tomatoes, tomato paste if you are using it, and simmer over low heat 20 minutes, stirring often. Add salt to taste.
6. Add lima beans, 3 cups of their liquid, and corn. Continue to simmer 10 to 15 minutes, stirring from time to time.
7. Grind in a generous amount of black pepper and adjust seasonings. Ladle into bowls and top with parsley. Serve hot.

1 tablespoon safflower oil
1 onion, chopped
6-8 cloves garlic, minced or put through a press
2 cups dried lima beans, washed, picked over, and soaked overnight
6 cups water
Sea salt, to taste
1 tablespoon olive oil
6 additional cloves garlic
1 teaspoon rosemary
1 teaspoon thyme
⅔ cup red wine
2 pounds ripe tomatoes, peeled and coarsely chopped or same amount canned tomatoes with their liquid, chopped
1 small can tomato paste if using fresh tomatoes
3 cups liquid from the beans
Kernels from 2-3 ears corn
Generous amount of freshly ground black pepper
2 tablespoons chopped fresh parsley

PASTA AND CHICKPEAS

Serves 6 to 8

2 cups chickpeas, soaked
6 cups water
1 onion, chopped
4 large cloves garlic,
    minced or put through a
    press
3 tablespoons olive oil
2 pounds ripe tomatoes or
    the equivalent canned,
    chopped
1 teaspoon fresh basil,
    chopped, or ½ teaspoon
    dried
½ teaspoon oregano
½-1 teaspoon crushed
    rosemary, to taste
Sea salt and freshly ground
    black pepper, to taste
1 small dried hot red pepper
1½ cups spiral pasta or
    macaroni
3 tablespoons fresh
    chopped parsley

1. Drain soaked beans. Combine with water in a large saucepan, bring to a boil, reduce heat, and cook 2 hours, or until soft. Add salt to taste. Do not drain.
2. Meanwhile make a tomato sauce. Heat 1 tablespoon of olive oil in a heavy-bottomed saucepan or large frying pan and add onion and 2 cloves of garlic.
3. Cook gently until onion is tender and add tomatoes. Stir together and simmer, uncovered, ½ hour, stirring occasionally.
4. Add oregano, basil, salt, and pepper and continue to cook 15 minutes. Add to beans and mix well.
5. Heat remaining olive oil and sauté remaining garlic and hot pepper over low heat until garlic begins to turn gold. Add to beans along with rosemary.
6. Let everything simmer together about 10 minutes. Make sure chickpeas are covered by at least 1 inch of liquid, and if they are not add a little more water. Taste and adjust seasonings.
7. Make sure chickpeas are simmering and stir in pasta. Cook until *al dente*. Stir in parsley and serve.

SOYBEAN 'GROUND BEEF'

*Although I normally avoid anything that calls itself a
"meat substitute", I can think of no better name for this
preparation, for it can be used to replace ground beef in so
many dishes, like spaghetti sauce, hamburgers, and
casseroles. It is savory and good, and I have fooled many a
meat eater with it.*

Serves 6

1. Soak soybeans overnight in water. In the
   morning grind them, a cup at a time, in a blender
   with onion, adding enough water to cover; you
   can use the soaking water.
2. Place ground soybeans in a very large saucepan,
   at least twice their volume. Add enough water to
   cover by 2 inches, and bring mixture slowly to a
   boil.
3. Add salt, reduce heat, and cover. Simmer 1 to 1½
   hours, or until the liquid is absorbed. (A thin
   layer may stick to the bottom of the pan, but it will
   come off easily with soaking.)

For the basic "ground
   soybeans":
1 cup dried soybeans
3 cups water
1 teaspoon sea salt
1 small onion

1. In a large, heavy-bottomed frying pan, sauté
   onion and garlic in oil until tender.
2. Add bouillon cubes and mash with the back of a
   spoon, then add tomato juice, Worcestershire
   sauce and soy sauce, and cook together a few
   minutes over medium heat.
3. Add soybeans and herbs. Stir together and cook,
   uncovered, over a medium flame until almost
   dry — about 40 minutes. Stir from time to time to
   prevent sticking. Remove from heat. This freezes
   well.

For the "ground beef":
1 onion, minced
*2 large cloves garlic,
   minced or put through a
   press*
1 tablespoon safflower oil
2 vegetable bouillon cubes
1 cup tomato juice
*1 tablespoon vegetarian
   Worcestershire sauce*
*1-2 tablespoons soy sauce,
   to taste*
*The cooked ground
   soybeans*
½ teaspoon thyme
½ teaspoon sage
½ teaspoon paprika

6

SIDE DISHES

POTATOES WITH PESTO

No book on herb cookery would be complete without this marvelous thick basil sauce. It is not only terrific with pasta but also as a sauce for potatoes, a dressing for a tomato salad, or a filling for mushrooms (see recipes).

Serves 4 to 6

2 cups fresh basil leaves
2 tablespoons pine nuts
2 large cloves garlic
Sea salt to taste
½ cup virgin olive oil
½ cup freshly grated
  Parmesan cheese
2 tablespoons freshly
  grated Romano cheese
2 pounds new or boiling
  potatoes
2 teaspoons butter
  (optional)

1. Place basil, pine nuts, garlic, and salt in a food processor fitted with the steel blade or in a blender. Turn on and pour in olive oil. Process until you have a fairly smooth paste. If you are using a blender you will have to stop and start it to stir down the mixture.
2. Remove from food processor or blender and stir in cheeses. Adjust salt, and set aside.
3. Cut potatoes into quarters and steam until tender. Drain and toss with pesto. If you wish, add a teaspoon or two of butter. Serve at once.

MUSHROOMS STUFFED WITH PESTO

Serves 4

1. Preheat oven to 400°F.
2. Make Pesto.
3. Clean mushrooms. Twist off stems and set aside for another use. Salt and pepper the inside of the mushroom caps.
4. Oil a baking dish with some of the olive oil. Place mushroom caps on it rounded side down, and fill open side of caps with Pesto. Drizzle on the rest of the olive oil and place in preheated oven.
5. Bake 15 to 20 minutes, basting occasionally with juices the mushrooms release. The mushrooms should be cooked through and the Pesto just beginning to brown on the top.

Note: The mushrooms can be cleaned, filled, and kept in the refrigerator for several hours.

1 batch Pesto (page 138)
16 very large or 20-24 smaller mushrooms
2 tablespoons olive oil
Sea salt and freshly ground black pepper

CARROTS WITH CARAWAY SEEDS

Serves 4

1. Steam carrots 5 to 10 minutes, or until crisp-tender. Refresh under cold water.
2. Heat safflower oil in a frying pan and add garlic. Sauté a minute or two and add carrots and caraway seeds. Stir-fry about 1 or 2 minutes, add salt and pepper to taste, and remove from heat. Transfer to a serving bowl, stir in yogurt, toss well, and serve.

1 pound carrots, sliced thin
1 tablespoon safflower oil
1 large clove garlic, minced or pressed
1 teaspoon crushed caraway seeds
Sea salt and freshly ground black pepper
1 cup plain yogurt

GREEK-STYLE WHITE BEANS

Serves 6 to 8

1 pound white beans,
  washed and soaked
1 tablespoon olive oil
1 onion, chopped
8 cloves garlic, peeled and
  crushed
5 cups water
1 bay leaf
1 teaspoon oregano
2 tablespoons tomato paste
Sea salt and freshly ground
  black pepper
Juice of 1 large lemon (more
  to taste)
½ cup chopped fresh
  parsley
½ red onion, minced
Additional garlic
  (optional)
Greek olives for garnish

1. Heat the tablespoon of olive oil in a large bean pot or soup pot and sauté onion until it begins to soften. Add garlic and sauté a few minutes longer.
2. Drain beans and add to the pot, along with water, bay leaf, oregano, and tomato paste. Bring to a boil, cover, reduce heat, and simmer 1 to 2 hours, or until beans are tender. Season to taste with sea salt and freshly ground pepper.
3. Remove beans from heat and add lemon juice, parsley, and chopped red onion. Add more garlic if you wish. Serve garnished with Greek black olives.
4. This can also be served cold. In that case, do not add lemon juice, parsley, and onion right away. Chill and add shortly before serving. Add more garlic if you wish, and garnish with olives.

BLACK OR PINTO BEANS WITH CORIANDER

*Fresh coriander is a typically Mexican addition to beans,
and ever since my first taste of beans seasoned with this
herb, years ago in a Mexican border town, black beans and
pintos just don't taste complete to me without it.*

1. Soak beans overnight or for several hours and drain.
2. Heat safflower oil in a large, heavy-bottomed soup pot or casserole and sauté onion with half the garlic until onion is tender. Add beans and water and bring to a boil. Reduce heat, cover, and simmer 1 hour.
3. Add remaining garlic and coriander. Add salt to taste and continue to cook another hour, or until beans are tender and broth thick and savory. You may wish to add more garlic or salt.
4. Serve with rice, tortillas, cornbread, or other whole grain bread.

*1 pound black or pinto
  beans, washed, picked
  over, and soaked
  overnight
1 tablespoon safflower oil
1 large onion, minced
4 large cloves garlic,
  minced or pressed
6 cups water
Sea salt to taste
3-4 tablespoons chopped
  fresh coriander*

Note: These can be frozen and will keep up to 3 days in the refrigerator.

KASHA WITH MUSHROOMS AND DILL

Serves 4 generously

2 ½ cups vegetable stock
1 cup buckwheat groats
1 egg, beaten
1 tablespoon safflower oil or
* butter (more as needed)*
1 small onion, chopped
½ pound mushrooms,
* cleaned and sliced*
Sea salt and freshly ground
* black pepper*
1 tablespoon brandy
* (optional)*
2 tablespoons chopped
* fresh dill*
Soy sauce to taste
* (optional)*
Plain yogurt for topping
* (optional)*

1. Have stock simmering in a saucepan.
2. Mix together buckwheat groats and egg in a bowl. Heat a dry saucepan over a medium flame and add groats. Cook, stirring, until all the egg is absorbed and grains are separate.
3. Add stock to groats. When it boils, cover, reduce heat, and cook 20 to 30 minutes, or until liquid is absorbed. Remove from heat.
4. Heat 1 tablespoon safflower oil or butter in a frying pan and add chopped onion. Sauté until onion is tender and add mushrooms. Cook, stirring, until they begin to soften and add salt, pepper, and brandy. Cook a minute, then add more butter or oil if necessary and stir in kasha and dill. Toss together until heated through, add soy sauce if you wish, and serve, topping with plain yogurt if desired.

PURÉE OF SWEET POTATOES WITH APPLE

Serves 4

1. Preheat oven to 425°F. Bake potatoes in their skins 40 to 45 minutes, or until thoroughly soft. At the same time, bake apples on a buttered baking sheet until soft — about 20 to 30 minutes.
2. Remove baked potatoes from their skins and core baked apples. Purée with yogurt, honey, lime juice, cinnamon, cloves, and nutmeg. Adjust seasonings.
3. Spoon or pipe on the sweet potato-apple purée onto the lemon-tossed apple rounds. Serve as a side dish.

1 pound sweet potatoes
1 pound apples
½ cup plain yogurt
1 tablespoon mild honey
1 tablespoon lime juice
½ teaspoon cinnamon
Ground cloves and freshly grated nutmeg to taste
2 additional apples, cut in rounds and tossed with lemon juice

ONIONS COOKED IN RED WINE

This is a dish to make on a day you plan to be home all afternoon.

Serves 6 to 8

1. Heat butter and oil over low heat in a heavy-bottomed, wide frying pan and sauté onions 1 hour, covered, stirring occasionally.
2. Uncover, add honey, and increase heat to medium high. Cook 25 minutes, stirring often, until onions are glazed and golden brown.
3. Reduce heat to low again, add wine and cook, stirring fairly often, 2 to 3 hours. The onions will be very soft, almost a purée, reddish brown and sweet. Add sea salt to taste. It takes a long time, but it's worth the effort. Serve as a side dish.

2 tablespoons safflower or vegetable oil
1 tablespoon butter
2 pounds yellow onions, sliced
2 tablespoons mild honey
1 ½ cups red wine
Sea salt to taste

COOKED CABBAGE WITH APPLES

Serves 4 to 6

1-2 tablespoons safflower
   or vegetable oil, as
   needed
1 onion, sliced
½ medium head red
   cabbage, shredded
2 cooking apples, peeled
   and sliced
2 tablespoons raisins
2 tablespoons mild honey
2 tablespoons red wine
   vinegar
½ teaspoon cinnamon
   (more to taste)
½ teaspoon allspice
½ teaspoon ground cloves
6 tablespoons plain low-fat
   yogurt

1. Heat safflower oil in a large, heavy-bottomed frying pan and brown onion.
2. Add red cabbage and apples and sauté about 3 minutes, stirring. Add raisins, honey, vinegar, cinnamon, allspice, and cloves and cook over medium heat, stirring from time to time, about 5 to 10 minutes. Remove from heat, let cool a moment, and stir in yogurt. Or transfer to a serving dish and then stir in yogurt. Serve with bulgur, couscous, or millet.

RATATOUILLE

A collection of my favourite recipes would not be complete without ratatouille, the slowly cooked vegetable stew from Provence. I have eaten the best ones in this region, and have concluded that in addition to the superb ingredients that grow in the area, the secret to these great ratatouilles is the earthenware pots in which they are cooked. These are easy enough to come by (they needn't be from Provence), and set over an asbestos pad they allow for the slow cooking that allows all of the heady aromas and flavors to develop to their utmost.

Serves 6

1. Salt diced eggplant and let sit while you prepare the other vegetables.
2. Heat oil over medium-low heat in a heavy-bottomed, preferably earthenware, casserole and gently sauté onions and garlic until onion is tender. Add sweet peppers and sauté for a few minutes.
3. Rinse eggplant and pat dry with a towel. Add to pot along with zucchini, and stir to coat thoroughly with oil. Add a bit more oil if necessary. Add some salt, cover pot, and cook over a very low heat 45 minutes to 1 hour, stirring from time to time.
4. Add tomatoes and herbs, and continue to cook, uncovered, another 10 to 15 minutes, stirring occasionally. Add salt to taste and plenty of freshly ground pepper. You may also want to add more herbs or a bit of cayenne pepper. Serve hot or cold. It is even better the next day. This freezes well.

1 pound eggplant, diced
2 onions, sliced
4 cloves garlic, sliced or chopped
3-4 tablespoons olive oil
2 sweet green or red peppers, seeded and sliced
1 pound zucchini, sliced, or if very large, diced
1 pound tomatoes, peeled and sliced
1 teaspoon thyme
1 tablespoon chopped fresh basil or 1 teaspoon dried
Sea salt and freshly ground black pepper, to taste

ARTICHOKES STEWED WITH TOMATOES AND WINE

Serves 4 to 6

4-6 artichokes
Juice of 1 lemon
1 tablespoon olive oil
1 small onion, minced
4 cloves garlic, minced
1 carrot, minced
1 stalk celery, minced
1 pound tomatoes, chopped
1 cup dry white wine
1 bay leaf
2 sprigs parsley
Sea salt and freshly ground
*   black pepper*

1. Trim artichokes, cut into quarters, remove chokes, and drop into a bowl of acidulated water (use the lemon juice for this).
2. Heat oil in a large, heavy-bottomed, lidded casserole and sauté onion with garlic, carrot, and celery until onion becomes translucent.
3. Add tomatoes and bring to a simmer. Cook for 5 minutes and add wine, bay leaf, parsley, salt and pepper, and artichokes.
4. Bring back to a simmer, cover, reduce heat, and simmer 40 minutes, or until artichokes are tender. Adjust seasonings and serve with the liquid spooned over artichokes.

PAN-FRIED MUSHROOMS

This is marvelous with Polenta (page 91) or over any cooked grains.

Serves 4

1. Heat butter in a large, heavy-bottomed frying pan and add onions or shallots. Sauté until they begin to soften, about 2 minutes, and add mushrooms and garlic.
2. Sauté over medium heat about 5 minutes and pour in wine.
3. Add herbs, turn up heat, and cook, stirring, until most of the wine has evaporated but you still have mushroom juices in the pan. Add salt and pepper to taste, remove from heat, and serve.

1-1½ pounds mushrooms, cleaned, trimmed, and sliced
1 tablespoon butter
5 scallions, white part only, or 2 medium shallots, minced
2 large cloves garlic, minced or put through a press
4 tablespoons dry white wine
½ teaspoon thyme
¼ teaspoon crushed rosemary
Sea salt and freshly ground black pepper, to taste
Additional herbs, to taste

ITALIAN-STYLE BROCCOLI

Serves 4 to 6

1. Steam broccoli 10 minutes, or until tender and still bright green. Refresh under cold water.
2. Heat olive oil over medium heat and sauté garlic and red pepper 2 minutes. Add broccoli and wine and sauté, stirring, another 3 to 5 minutes. Serve.

1½-2 pounds broccoli, broken into florets
1 tablespoon olive oil
1 clove garlic, minced or put through a press
1 small dried hot red pepper, crumbled
2 tablespoons dry white wine

ROASTED EGGPLANT WITH GARLIC AND HERBS

Serves 4 to 6

3 medium eggplants
3 cloves garlic, minced
½ cup chopped fresh
  parsley
1 teaspoon chopped fresh
  rosemary or ½ teaspoon
  crumbled dried
  rosemary
Sea salt and freshly ground
  black pepper, to taste
3 tablespoons olive oil
Lemon juice, to taste
Thin slices of lemon, for
  garnish

1. Cut the eggplant in half lengthwise, and make two lengthwise slits down the cut side of each half.
2. Mix together garlic, parsley, and rosemary, add freshly ground pepper, and fill slits with this mixture. Salt eggplant lightly and drizzle on some olive oil. Cover and chill 2 hours.
3. Make a wood or charcoal fire, or preheat oven to 350°F. When the fire dies down, grill eggplant, basting regularly with olive oil, until tender. Or place cut side down in an oiled baking dish and bake 1 hour, basting from time to time, in preheated oven. Turn eggplant cut side up for the last quarter hour and baste with juices in pan.
4. Sprinkle on some lemon juice, garnish with thin rounds of lemon, and serve.

BAKED WHOLE TOMATOES À LA PROVENÇALE

Serves 4 to 6

1. Preheat oven to 400°F.
2. Cut tomatoes across the top, about ½-inch down from stem. Gently scoop out seeds and place upside-down on a rack for 10 minutes.
3. Mix together shallots, garlic, and herbs. Place tomatoes cut side up on an oiled baking sheet or in an oiled baking pan.
4. Lightly salt and pepper, and sprinkle with herbs and garlic mixture, then with breadcrumbs.
5. Drizzle on a little olive oil and bake 10 minutes. They should be cooked through but still hold their shape. Remove from heat and serve.

4-6 firm, large, ripe tomatoes
2 cloves garlic, minced
2 shallots, minced
2 tablespoons chopped fresh parsley
2 tablespoons chopped fresh basil, if available (Do not substitute dried.)
½ teaspoon thyme
¼ teaspoon crushed rosemary
Sea salt and freshly ground black pepper
3 tablespoons whole wheat breadcrumbs
Olive oil

GREEN BEANS AMANDINE

Serves 4

1. Steam beans 10 minutes. Refresh under cold water.
2. Heat butter and sauté almonds with garlic until they begin to turn color.
3. Add beans and continue to sauté another 3 minutes or so, or until completely heated through. Add salt and freshly ground pepper to taste, and serve.

1 pound tender green beans, trimmed
2 tablespoons butter
½ cup slivered almonds
1 clove garlic, minced or put through a press
Sea salt and freshly ground black pepper, to taste

POTATO GRATIN WITH GARLIC

Serves 6

2 pounds boiling potatoes
6 cloves garlic, thinly sliced
2 tablespoons butter
Sea salt and freshly ground black pepper, to taste
1 cup grated Gruyère cheese
1 cup boiling milk

1. Preheat oven to 425°F.
2. Wash potatoes and slice ½-inch thick. Place in a bowl of cold water as you do this. When they are all sliced, drain and dry in a towel.
3. Butter a 2-inch deep 10-inch flameproof gratin or baking dish. Layer half the potatoes and dot with half the garlic slices, half the butter, some salt and freshly ground pepper, and half the grated cheese. Repeat layers and pour on boiling milk.
4. Set over medium heat and bring to a simmer. Place in upper third of oven and bake for 30 minutes, or until milk has been absorbed and top is browned. Serve.

GREEN BEANS À LA PROVENÇALE

Serves 6

1. Steam beans 5 to 10 minutes and refresh under cold water.
2. Heat oil in a large saucepan and add tomatoes and garlic. Simmer over medium-high heat 10 minutes.
3. Add beans, herbs, and salt and pepper to taste, cover, reduce heat to medium-low, and cook another 10 minutes. Stir from time to time.
4. Remove from heat and serve.

1½ pounds green beans, trimmed
1 tablespoon olive oil
1 pound ripe tomatoes, chopped
2 cloves garlic, minced or put through a press
½ teaspoon thyme
1 tablespoon chopped fresh basil or 1 teaspoon dried
Sea salt and freshly ground black pepper, to taste

SAUTÉED CABBAGE AND ONIONS WITH GARLIC

Serves 4

1. Heat oil in a large, heavy-bottomed frying pan or wok. Add onion and sauté over medium heat until it begins to brown.
2. Add garlic and continue to sauté another 5 minutes.
3. Add soy sauce, sesame seeds, and cabbage and stir-fry 5 to 10 minutes over medium-high heat, adding more oil if necessary. Serve with grains.

2 tablespoons safflower or vegetable oil
1 large onion, cut in half and sliced in thin strips
2 cloves garlic, minced or put through a press
1 tablespoon soy sauce
1 tablespoon sesame seeds
1 pound shredded red or white cabbage

114

TURNIPS WITH PARSLEY AND BREADCRUMBS

Serves 4 to 6

2 pounds turnips
1 tablespoon olive oil
1 clove garlic, minced or
   put through a press
4 tablespoons whole wheat
   breadcrumbs
3 tablespoons chopped
   fresh parsley
Sea salt and freshly ground
   black pepper, to taste

1. Try to find small, young turnips. Peel, cut in half if large, place in a steamer above boiling water, cover, and steam 10 minutes. Drain and refresh under cold water. Cut into quarters.
2. Heat olive oil in a frying pan and sauté garlic until golden — about 1 minute.
3. Add turnips and turn heat to low. Cover and cook about 10 minutes, shaking pan occasionally to make sure they don't stick.
4. Add breadcrumbs and parsley and continue to cook until oil is absorbed and breadcrumbs crisp. Season to taste with salt and freshly ground pepper.

LENTILS WITH HERB BUTTER

Serves 6

2 cups lentils
1 small onion, chopped
2 cloves garlic, minced or
   put through a press
1 bay leaf
Sea salt, to taste
Freshly ground black
   pepper
4 tablespoons Herb Butter
   (page 164)

1. Soak lentils in 3 times their volume of water 1 hour and drain.
2. Combine lentils, onion, garlic, and bay leaf in a large saucepan and add water to cover by 2 inches. Bring to a boil, add salt to taste, reduce heat, cover, and simmer 45 minutes, or until lentils are tender. Pour off stock, if much remains, stir in plenty of black pepper, and stir in Herb Butter. Serve.

BROWN RICE AND GARLIC

If you wish, soak the rice for an hour in 3 times its volume of water. This optional step renders the grains a little more tender.

Serves 6

1. Heat oil in a heavy-bottomed saucepan and sauté garlic 2 minutes, or until it begins to turn color.
2. Add rice and sauté a minute or two, until thoroughly coated with oil. Add water and bring to a boil. Add salt, reduce heat, and cover.
3. Simmer 35 minutes and check to see if water has been absorbed. If not, simmer another 10 minutes without disturbing. If so, add a further 4 tablespoons boiling water and simmer, covered, for another 5 to 10 minutes.
4. Let sit, covered, 10 minutes off the heat, then fluff and serve with soy sauce or a little butter.

1 cup raw brown rice, washed
1 tablespoon safflower oil
6 cloves garlic, lightly crushed, skins removed
2 cups water
½ teaspoon sea salt (or to taste)
Soy sauce or butter

Note: Feel free to use more or less garlic here, according to your taste. Also, millet could be substituted for the rice. If so, before heating the oil in the pan, toast the millet over dry heat just until it begins to smell fragrant, and remove from the heat.

7

SALADS

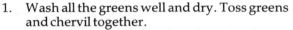

SALADE MESCLUN (MIXED GREENS SALAD)

Serves 4 to 6

½ pound mixed tender
  bitter greens, such as
  lamb's lettuce, chicory,
  dandelion greens,
  nasturtium, oak leaf
  lettuce, watercress
1 ounce chervil, stems
  included
2 tablespoons good quality
  wine vinegar
Sea salt and freshly ground
  black pepper
1 small clove garlic
  (optional)
½ teaspoon Dijon mustard
  (optional)
6 tablespoons olive oil or 4
  tablespoons safflower oil
  and 2 tablespoons
  walnut oil

1. Wash all the greens well and dry. Toss greens
    and chervil together.
2. Combine vinegar, sea salt and pepper, the
    optional garlic and mustard, and the oil or oils.
    Mix together well and toss with salad. Serve at
    once.

TOMATO AND MOZZARELLA SALAD WITH PESTO

Serves 4 to 6

1. Make Pesto and set aside (freeze half if you make a whole batch).
2. Stir additional olive oil into Pesto you are using.
3. Slice tomatoes in thin lengthwise slices, from stem end down to within about ¼ inch of bottom.
4. Slice Mozzarella very thin, and insert between tomato slices. Grind some pepper over the top.
5. Line individual salad plates with lettuce leaves or watercress. Place tomatoes on top and drizzle on Pesto. Serve.

½ recipe Pesto (page 138)
4 additional tablespoons olive oil
4-6 firm, ripe, medium-sized tomatoes
4 ounces Mozzarella cheese
Freshly ground black pepper
Fresh basil leaves for garnish
Watercress or lettuce leaves for lining plates

CARAWAY COLESLAW

Serves 6 to 8

1. Prepare vegetables and apples and toss together in a bowl, along with crushed caraway seeds.
2. Heat honey and cider vinegar together in a small saucepan, just until honey dissolves into vinegar. Add lemon juice. Remove from heat and stir in yogurt. Mix well.
3. Toss dressing with cabbage mixture. Add freshly ground pepper to taste, cover, and refrigerate overnight.

½ medium head green cabbage, finely shredded
2 apples, grated
2 stalks celery, thinly sliced
½ medium onion, grated
1 teaspoon crushed caraway seeds
1 carrot, grated (optional)
¼ cup cider vinegar
½ cup mild honey
1½ cups plain yogurt
¼ cup lemon juice
Freshly ground black pepper

LEBANESE EGGPLANT SALAD

Serves 4 to 6

1 pound eggplant
Olive oil
3 tablespoons tahini
Juice of 1 lemon
1-2 cloves garlic, minced or
    pressed
Cayenne to taste (1-2
    pinches)
Sea salt to taste
Fresh chopped parsley for
    ganish
1 red or green pepper,
    sliced in wide strips

1. Preheat oven to 450°F. Cut eggplant in half lengthwise and score with a sharp knife down the middle, to the skin but not through it. Oil a baking sheet with olive oil and place eggplant on it, cut side down. Bake in the hot oven 15 to 20 minutes, or until thoroughly soft and the skin is shrivelled. Remove from oven and allow to cool.
2. Scoop the eggplant out from skin and mash in a mortar and pestle, or in a food processor. Blend in tahini, lemon juice, garlic, cayenne, and sea salt. Place in an attractive bowl and sprinkle with parsley. Chill.
3. Serve, using strips of green or red peppers as scoopers.

BEET SALAD

Serves 4

1 pound raw beets
2 tablespoons chopped
    fresh parsley or dill
1 cup plain yogurt
1 clove garlic, puréed or
    put through a press
1 teaspoon crushed
    caraway seeds
Sea salt and freshly ground
    black pepper

1. Steam beets until tender, 15 to 30 minutes, depending on size of beets. Drain, run under cold water, and remove skin. Slice thinly, and toss with parsley or dill.
2. Mix together yogurt, garlic, caraway seeds sea salt, and freshly ground pepper. Toss with beets and serve, or chill and serve.

CAROTTES RAPÉES (GRATED CARROT SALAD)

This is a very simple French salad, and one of my favorites.

Serves 4 to 6

1. Grate carrots fine, either with a hand grater or a food processor. Toss them with chives and parsley.
2. Combine lemon juice, vinegar, garlic, Dijon mustard, salt, and pepper and mix together well. Whisk in oil or oils and toss with carrots. Serve at once or chill and serve, tossing once more just before serving.

2 pounds carrots
2 tablespoons chopped chives
1-2 tablespoons chopped fresh parsley
Juice of ½ lemon
1 tablespoon wine vinegar
1 small clove garlic, minced
1 teaspoon Dijon mustard
Sea salt and freshly ground black pepper
8 tablespoons olive oil, or a mixture of olive oil and safflower oil

MELON, CUCUMBER, AND TOMATO SALAD

This may seem strange at first glance, but it works quite well.

Serves 6

For the salad:
1 large cucumber, peeled and diced
1 pound ripe tomatoes
1 honeydew melon
1 tablespoon chopped fresh parsley
1 tablespoon chopped fresh mint
1½ tablespoons chopped chives

For the dressing:
3 tablespoons wine vinegar
½-1 teaspoon mild honey
Sea salt and freshly ground black pepper
6 tablespoons safflower or vegetable oil
Fresh watercress for garnish

1. Salt cucumber pieces and let sit 1 hour.
2. Peel and seed tomatoes and cut into wedges, and peel melon and cut into 1-inch dice, or make into balls.
3. Rinse cucumber thoroughly and toss together with melon and tomatoes.
4. Mix together vinegar, honey, sea salt, and freshly ground pepper. Whisk in oil and toss with salad mixture. Place in a glass salad bowl and chill 1 to 2 hours.
5. Just before serving toss with herbs. Garnish with watercress and serve.

RED CABBAGE AND APPLE SALAD WITH POPPY SEED DRESSING

Serves 4 to 6

1. Make salad dressing.
2. Toss together cabbage, apple, and chives. Toss with dressing.
3. Line a salad bowl or platter with lettuce leaves and fill with salad. Serve, or chill and serve.

1 recipe Poppy Seed
    Dressing (page 146)
1 pound red cabbage,
    shredded
1 apple, grated
2 tablespoons minced
    chives
Leaf lettuce for the bowl or
    platter

MIDDLE EASTERN SALAD

Serves 4 to 6

1. Toss together all the ingredients for the salad.
2. Mix together lemon juice, garlic, yogurt, sea salt, and pepper and whisk in olive oil.
3. Toss salad with dressing and serve. You may chill this for an hour or so, but no longer.

½ medium cucumber,
    cubed
4 scallions, thinly sliced
4 tomatoes, chopped
1 green or red pepper, diced
1 bunch watercress,
    chopped
2 tablespoons chopped
    fresh dill

For the dressing:
3 tablespoons lemon juice
1 clove garlic, minced or
    pressed
2 tablespoons yogurt
Sea salt and freshly ground
    black pepper
¼ cup olive oil

LENTIL SALAD

Serves 6

1 tablespoon safflower or
    vegetable oil
1 onion, chopped
2 cloves garlic, minced or
    pressed
1 pound lentils, washed
Water to cover lentils by 2
    inches
1 bay leaf
3 tablespoons wine vinegar
1 additional clove garlic,
    puréed
½ teaspoon Dijon mustard
1 teaspoon ground cumin
Sea salt and freshly ground
    black pepper
½ cup olive oil
Cooking liquid from the
    lentils
1 red onion, minced
½ bunch chopped fresh
    parsley
Leaf lettuce and tomatoes
    for garnish

1. Heat safflower or vegetable oil in a heavy-bottomed saucepan and sauté onion and 1 clove garlic until onion is tender. Add lentils, water, the remaining clove of garlic, and the bay leaf. Bring to a boil, reduce heat, cover, and cook until lentils are tender, about 45 minutes. Remove the bay leaf. Remove from heat and drain, retaining liquid.

2. Mix together vinegar, additional garlic, mustard, cumin, salt, and freshly ground pepper. Whisk in olive oil. Add cooking liquid from lentils to taste.

3. Toss dressing with lentils and stir in red onion and parsley. Cover and chill. Serve over a bed of lettuce leaves, with sliced tomatoes for garnish.

ZUCCHINI WITH YOGURT AND MINT

Serves 4

1. Cut zucchini into spears and steam 5 to 10 minutes, to taste. Refresh under cold water and pat dry.
2. Toss steamed zucchini with yogurt and mint. Add sea salt to taste. Refrigerate until ready to serve.

1 pound zucchini
1½ cups plain yogurt
2-3 tablespoons chopped mint
Sea salt to taste

ROMAINE AND MUSHROOM SALAD WITH FENNEL

Serves 4 to 6

1. Separate lettuce leaves, wash and slice crosswise.
2. Using a lemon peeler or sharp knife, pare rind from half the lemon and trim away any white part. Slice the trimmed peel into very fine shreds, blanch, and drain.
3. Cut away white pith from lemon by working a serrated knife around in a spiral with a sawing motion, the blade angled in slightly. Now cut away thin slices of lemon flesh from in between membranes. Toss these with romaine, fennel seeds, mushrooms, and chopped fennel.
4. Combine lemon juice, vinegar, mustard, salt, pepper, and honey. Whisk in oil, then cream or buttermilk. Adjust seasonings, toss with salad, and serve, garnishing with radishes.

1 head romaine lettuce
1 thick-skinned lemon
1 teaspoon crushed fennel seeds
¼ pound mushrooms, sliced
2 tablespoons chopped fresh fennel
Radishes for garnish

For the dressing:
Juice of ½ lemon
1-2 tablespoons tarragon vinegar
¼ teaspoon dry mustard
Sea salt and freshly ground black pepper
½ teaspoon honey
3 tablespoons safflower oil
3 tablespoons cream or buttermilk

WARM GREEN BEAN AMANDINE SALAD

Serves 4 to 6

1½ pounds green beans
½ cup slivered almonds
1 tablespoon butter or
    safflower oil
Juice of ½ lemon
2 tablespoons red wine or
    champagne vinegar
½-1 teaspoon Dijon
    mustard, to taste
1 small clove garlic, minced
    or put through a press
¼ teaspoon tarragon
¼ teaspoon marjoram
½ cup olive oil, or a
    combination of olive and
    safflower oil
4 tablespoons chopped
    fresh parsley
Sea salt and freshly ground
    black pepper, to taste

1. Steam green beans until just tender — about 10 minutes. Sauté almonds in butter or oil until brown.
2. Make a vinaigrette with lemon juice, vinegar, mustard, garlic, herbs, and oil.
3. When beans are done, drain and toss at once with dressing, almonds, and chopped fresh parsley. Add salt and freshly ground pepper to taste and serve at once.

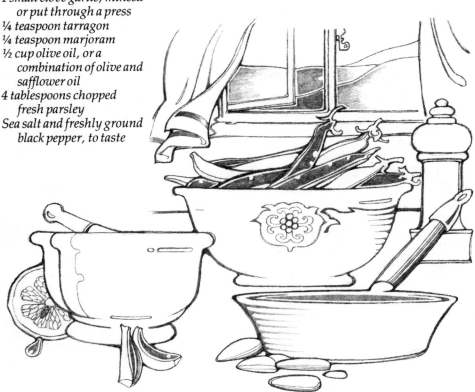

ROASTED RED PEPPER SALAD

Serves 4 to 6

1. Heat broiler and place peppers on a baking sheet close to flame. Roast, turning at regular intervals, until peppers are charred black all the way around. (This can also be done directly over a flame, turning the peppers regularly.)
2. Remove peppers from heat and place in a damp towel or in a plastic bag for 10 minutes. Peel off all of charred skin under cold water. Pat dry with paper towels.
3. Cut peppers in half, remove seeds and membranes, and cut into wide strips.
4. Mix together olive oil, garlic, salt and pepper to taste, and toss with peppers.
5. Refrigerate, covered, 1 hour before serving. Garnish, if you wish, with fresh basil.

2-4 large sweet red peppers
5 tablespoons olive oil
1 clove garlic, minced, puréed, or put through a press
Sea salt and freshly ground black pepper, to taste
Fresh chopped basil (optional)

TOMATO AND RED ONION SALAD WITH GOAT CHEESE

Serves 4

1. Layer tomato slices attractively on a platter and top with onions and goat cheese.
2. Mix together vinegar, garlic, salt, and freshly ground pepper, and stir in olive oil.
3. Pour over salad, and garnish with basil. Scatter olives on salad and serve.

4 large, ripe tomatoes, sliced thin
1 medium red onion, sliced in thin rings
3 ounces goat cheese, sliced
1 tablespoon red wine vinegar
1 clove garlic, minced
Sea salt and freshly ground black pepper, to taste
3-4 tablespoons fruity olive oil
Imported French olives and fresh basil, for garnish

TABOULI

Serves 6 to 8

1⅓ cups bulghur
Juice of 2 lemons
1 clove garlic, minced or
    put through a press (or
    more, to taste)
½ teaspoon ground cumin
Sea salt to taste
½ cup olive oil
2 large, ripe tomatoes,
    chopped
1 cup chopped fresh parsley
1 small cucumber, peeled
    and chopped
4 tablespoons minced
    scallions
4 tablespoons chopped
    fresh mint
Crisp inner leaves from 1
    head romaine lettuce

1. Place bulghur in a bowl and pour on three times its volume of water. Let it soak 1 hour, or until soft.
2. Place a tea towel in a colander and drain bulghur. Squeeze out excess moisture in towel, and place bulghur in a bowl.
3. Mix together lemon juice, garlic, cumin, and salt to taste. Stir in olive oil and blend well.
4. Toss with bulghur, tomatoes, parsley, cucumber, minced scallions, and mint. Decorate bowl with lettuce leaves, which you can use as scoopers. This salad should be served with pita bread.

CAULIFLOWER VINAIGRETTE WITH PEAS

Serves 6

1. Bring a large pot of water to a boil and drop in sliced onion.
2. Add cauliflower, and when water comes back to a boil, time for 2 minutes, then drain. Refresh under cold water and drain on a towel.
3. Steam peas 10 minutes, or until tender but still bright green. Refresh under cold water and drain on a towel.
4. Toss vegetables and herbs together with Mild Vinaigrette and chill until ready to serve, or serve at once.

1 red onion, sliced very thin
1 large head cauliflower, broken into florets
1 pound fresh peas, shelled (unshelled weight)
4 tablespoons chopped fresh parsley
1 tablespoon chopped fresh tarragon, if available
1 recipe Mild Vinaigrette (page 148)

CUCUMBER-YOGURT SALAD

Serves 6

1. Mix together vinegar, lemon juice, garlic, mustard, herbs, salt, and pepper.
2. Stir in yogurt, whisk together until you have a smooth sauce, and toss with cucumbers and onions. Chill and toss again before serving.

4 tablespoons wine vinegar
Juice of ½ lemon
1 clove garlic, minced, puréed, or put through a press
1 teaspoon Dijon mustard
1 teaspoon fresh chopped herbs, such as basil, parsley, thyme
Sea salt and freshly ground black pepper, to taste
½ cup plain yogurt
2 pounds cucumbers, peeled and sliced thin
1 small red onion, sliced thin

CUCUMBER AND TOMATO SALAD IN GARLIC-YOGURT DRESSING

Serves 6

1 large cucumber or 2
  smaller ones, peeled and
  chopped
½ pound tomatoes,
  chopped
4 scallions, minced
½ cup chopped fresh mint
½ cup chopped fresh
  parsley
Juice of 2 large lemons
2 cloves garlic, minced or
  put through a press
Sea salt, to taste
2 tablespoons olive oil
1 cup plain low-fat yogurt
Freshly ground black
  pepper

1. Toss together vegetables and herbs.
2. Stir together lemon juice, garlic, salt, olive oil, and yogurt until smooth. Grind in some pepper.
3. Toss with vegetables and serve, or chill and serve.

SHREDDED VEGETABLE SALAD WITH SPICY CHINESE DRESSING

Serves 6

1. Combine all the shredded vegetables and toss with dressing.
2. Line a platter or salad bowl with lettuce leaves, and fill with shredded vegetable mixture.
3. Sprinkle top with additional sesame seeds and chopped fresh coriander, and serve.

1 pound shredded cabbage
1 small or medium cucumber, peeled and shredded or cut in julienne strips
1 medium or large carrot, shredded
3 scallions, chopped
2 tablespoons toasted sesame seeds
1 recipe Oriental Salad Dressing (page 143)
1 head Bibb lettuce, leaves separated and washed
Chopped fresh coriander and additional sesame seeds for garnish

MARINATED CUCUMBERS

Serves 6 to 8

2 large or 3-4 smaller
    cucumbers, peeled and
    cut into spears
1 white or red onion, sliced
    thin
¾ cup water
¾ cup white wine or cider
    vinegar
2 cloves garlic, minced or
    put through a press
Sea salt and freshly ground
    black pepper, to taste
2 tablespoons chopped
    fresh dill, or 1
    tablespoon dried
4 tablespoons safflower oil

1. Combine onion, vinegar, water, and garlic in a saucepan and bring to a boil. Boil 1 minute and remove from heat.
2. Cool 1 minute, and add salt and pepper, dill, and oil. Pour over cucumbers and toss well.
3. Cover and refrigerate several hours, tossing from time to time.

8

DRESSINGS AND SAUCES

TOMATO SAUCE WITH BASIL

Makes 5 cups

1. Seed and chop tomatoes.
2. Heat olive oil or butter in a heavy-bottomed wide frying pan or a saucepan and add onion and 2 cloves of the garlic. Sauté a few minutes, or until onion is tender.
3. Add tomatoes, remaining garlic, and tomato paste and bring to a simmer. Turn up heat and cook quickly for 20 minutes, stirring from time to time.
4. Add salt and freshly ground pepper to taste, and the basil. Cook another 5 minutes and taste. If you want a sweeter sauce, add a pinch of cinnamon. Correct salt, pepper, and garlic and remove from heat.
5. Use in pasta dishes or with grains.

Use fresh tomatoes only if you can find very ripe local tomatoes. Otherwise, canned will yield a much better sauce.

Note: This sauce can be frozen and keeps several days in the refrigerator.

3 pounds fresh or canned
    tomatoes*
1 tablespoon olive oil or
    butter
1 small onion, minced
3 cloves garlic, minced or
    put through a press
1 tablespoon tomato paste
    (optional)
2 tablespoons fresh
    chopped basil
Sea salt and freshly ground
    black pepper to taste
Pinch of cinnamon
    (optional)

HERB VINEGARS

Any number of vinegars can be infused with fresh herbs to give you a variety of salad dressings and sauces. I most often use tarragon and mint for my flavored vinegars, but basil is also good, and fresh coriander and dill make interesting vinegars as well.

1-3 sprigs tarragon, mint, or basil
1 quart wine or cider vinegar

1. Combine herbs and vinegar in a jar and seal well. Allow to macerate for 2 weeks before using.
2. You can also fill a jar with loosely packed leaves of the herbs, cover with vinegar, macerate for 2 weeks, and strain.

CORIANDER-CUMIN TOMATO SAUCE

1 large bunch fresh coriander, about 1 ounce
6 heaping tablespoons parsley
1 seeded green chili
2 scallions or shallots, trimmed
1 large clove garlic
3 tablespoons olive oil
1½ teaspoons ground cumin
1 pound tomatoes, peeled, and chopped
1 tablespoon tomato paste
Sea salt to taste

1. Using a blender or food processor with the steel blade, blend together coriander, parsley, chili, scallions or shallots, garlic, and two tablespoons of olive oil. Set aside.
2. Heat oil in a heavy frying pan and add cumin. Turn heat high, cook a few seconds, and add chopped tomatoes. Cook for 1 to 2 minutes over high heat, stirring or shaking the pan. Stir in tomato paste, cook about half a minute more, and remove from heat. Allow to cool and stir into coriander mixture. Add salt to taste.
3. Cover and refrigerate before serving. Use as a dip or as a hot sauce, or as a dressing with avocados.

Note: This can be frozen and will keep for a few days in the refrigerator.

CORIANDER SAUCE

1. Cover prunes with water and bring to a simmer. Simmer ½ hour, or until thoroughly soft. Drain and retain ½ cup of liquid for sauce.
2. Combine all ingredients except oil and cooking liquid from prunes in a blender or food processor fitted with the steel blade and blend together until you have a paste. Without stopping the blender or food processor, blend in oil and liquid. Adjust seasonings. Use as a dip, as a topping for tofu or grains, or as a sauce for vegetables.

Can use all coriander.

Note: This will last for about 3 days in the refrigerator.

4-6 pitted prunes
½ cup cooking liquid from the prunes (see Step 1)
4 tablespoons lime juice
¾ cup fresh coriander leaves
½ cup chopped fresh parsley
¼ cup chopped fresh basil*
2 cloves garlic, peeled
½ teaspoon chopped fresh ginger
¼-½ teaspoon sea salt
¼ teaspoon freshly ground black pepper
4 tablespoons sunflower seeds
4 tablespoons walnut or safflower oil

VERY QUICK, VERY FRESH TOMATO SAUCE

Use only the ripest tomatoes for this sauce. It is a nice accompaniment for eggs or pasta. Also good with vegetables like zucchini, green beans or eggplant.

Makes 2 cups

1 tablespoon butter or olive oil
1 shallot, minced
1 clove garlic, minced
1 pound tomatoes, peeled and chopped
2 teaspoons chopped fresh marjoram
Sea salt and freshly ground black pepper

1. Heat butter or oil in a heavy-bottomed frying pan and sauté shallot and garlic gently for 2 minutes, or until shallot is soft. Add tomatoes, turn heat to moderately high, and cook 10 to 15 minutes. Add marjoram and sea salt and freshly ground pepper to taste, remove from heat, and serve.

Note: This can be frozen, but in that case cook 30 minutes.

TOFU TOMATO SAUCE

Makes about 1½ quarts

1 tablespoon olive or safflower oil
1 onion, minced
3 cloves garlic, minced or pressed
½ pound tofu
1 tablespoon tamari soy sauce
3 pounds tomatoes, seeded and puréed, or the equivalent canned
3 tablespoons tomato paste
1 teaspoon dried oregano
Pinch of thyme
½ teaspoon mild honey
Sea salt and freshly ground black pepper
Pinch of cinnamon

1. Heat oil in a large, heavy-bottomed frying pan or saucepan and sauté onion with 1 clove of the garlic until onion is tender.
2. Add tamari, tofu, and more oil if necessary, and cook, mashing tofu with back of your spoon, until tofu begins to stick to pan, about 5 to 10 minutes. Add tomatoes and remaining ingredients and bring to a simmer. Cook, covered, 30 minutes. Adjust seasonings.
3. Remove from heat and serve with pasta, grains, or vegetables.

Note: This will keep a few days in the refrigerator but will not freeze.

GARLICKY TOMATO AND CAPER SAUCE

Serves 4 to 6

1. Heat olive oil in a large, heavy-bottomed frying pan and add onion.
2. Sauté a few minutes and add garlic and capers. Sauté, stirring, 5 minutes, and add tomatoes.
3. Cook over moderate heat, stirring occasionally, ½ hour. Season to taste with freshly ground pepper.
4. Serve this with pasta, such as fettuccine or tagliatelli, or as an accompaniment to zucchini.

1 tablespoon olive oil
1 small or ½ medium onion, finely chopped
1 cup capers, chopped in a food processor or mashed in a mortar and pestle
1 small head garlic, cloves separated and peeled, then put through a press or chopped and blended with the capers in a food processor or mortar and pestle
2 ½ pounds tomatoes, chopped
Freshly ground black pepper, to taste

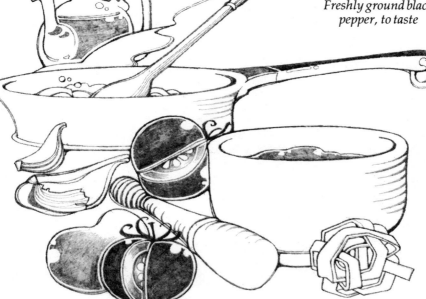

TOMATO COULIS

Makes 2½ cups

2 pounds tomatoes, cut in
    half lengthwise
1 clove garlic, minced or
    put through a press
1 onion, cut in half
2 tablespoons butter
Sea salt, to taste
Pinch of cinnamon

1. Simmer tomatoes in a lidded, heavy-bottomed saucepan 10 minutes.
2. Purée through a food mill and return to pan. Add butter, onion, garlic, and salt.
3. Cook at a slow, steady simmer 1 hour. Add a pinch of cinnamon and discard onion. Adjust salt.
4. Serve with vegetables, thin pasta, grains, or ravioli.

RICH TOMATO SAUCE

Makes 1 quart

1 tablespoon olive oil
1 large onion, chopped
4 large cloves garlic,
    minced or put through a
    press (or more to taste)
1 small carrot, minced
3 pounds tomatoes, seeded
    and chopped
1-2 small cans tomato
    paste, to taste
1 bay leaf
1 teaspoon dried basil or 1
    tablespoon fresh,
    chopped
1-2 teaspoons oregano, to
    taste
Sea salt and freshly ground
    black pepper, to taste
Pinch of cinnamon

1. Heat oil in a heavy-bottomed saucepan and sauté onion, 2 cloves of garlic, and carrot until onion is tender.
2. Add tomatoes, remaining garlic, tomato paste, and bay leaf and bring to a simmer.
3. Simmer, covered, 1 to 2 hours, stirring occasionally. Remove bay leaf and add basil and oregano.
4. Simmer another 15 minutes and add salt and freshly ground pepper to taste, and a pinch or two of cinnamon. (Add more garlic if desired.)
5. This is good for lasagnes, pizzas and lusty pasta dishes. It freezes well.

BLENDER "BÉARNAISE"

It is the vinegar reduction which allows me to call this sauce a béarnaise, for it has none of the butter and eggs of a traditional one. It is tart and savory, and goes well with vegetables and grains.

1. Combine vinegar, shallot, carrot, and celery in a small, heavy-bottomed saucepan and place over moderate heat. Simmer mixture until almost all of the vinegar has evaporated. There should only be enough left so that vegetables aren't completely dry.
2. Add chopped tomato and continue to cook, stirring occasionally, for about 15 minutes, or until the mixture is almost dry again. About 5 minutes before the end of this cooking, stir in parsley.
3. Remove from heat and transfer to a blender. Blend, along with vegetable stock, until smooth. While blender is running, drizzle in olive oil.
4. Transfer puréed sauce back to saucepan season to taste with sea salt and freshly ground pepper and tarragon. Heat through gently and serve. This can also be served cold.

Note: This sauce freezes well and will keep for a few days in the refrigerator.

4 tablespoons tarragon
   vinegar
6 tablespoons minced
   shallot or scallion
   bottoms
3 tablespoons minced
   carrot
3 tablespoons minced celery
1 large ripe tomato, peeled,
   seeded, and chopped
2 tablespoons chopped
   parsley
½ cup vegetable stock
1 tablespoon olive oil
1 teaspoon chopped fresh
   tarragon
Sea salt and freshly ground
   black pepper

PESTO

If you've never had this heady mixture of basil, garlic, and cheese be prepared for a taste treat that will change your life. It is traditionally tossed with pasta, but I like it as a topping for tomatoes, as well as potatoes and other vegetables. This keeps in the refrigerator for about a week, and you can freeze it by omitting the cheese and adding it when thawed.

Serves 6

1 tightly packed cup fresh
    basil leaves
2 large cloves garlic, peeled
3 tablespoons pine nuts or
    broken walnuts
A little sea salt
½ cup olive oil
¾ cup freshly grated
    Parmesan cheese (or
    more, to taste)

1. Using a blender or food processor, combine basil, garlic, salt, and nuts and pulse several times to begin chopping and blending ingredients. Scrape blades often.
2. Now turn on machine at high speed and add olive oil in a slow, steady stream. Blend until you have a smooth paste. You may have to stop blender and clean blades occasionally.
3. Transfer mixture to a bowl and stir in Parmesan. Adjust seasonings.
4. This can also be made in a mortar and pestle. Pound together basil, garlic, salt, and nuts until you have a paste, then blend in olive oil a little at a time, and stir in cheese.

TAHINI-TAMARI SAUCE

6 tablespoons tahini
2 tablespoons tamari soy
    sauce
2 tablespoons warm water
½ teaspoon ground ginger,
    or 1 teaspoon grated
    fresh
2 teaspoons mild honey

Combine all the ingredients in a bowl and stir together well. Refrigerate. Use this as a spread for bread or tofu or as a dip for raw vegetables.

TOFU REMOULADE SAUCE

This makes a spectacular low-fat dressing for vegetable salads. It will keep for up to a week in the refrigerator.

Blend all the ingredients except tarragon, chives, and capers together in a blender or food processor until smooth. Stir in herbs and capers. Chill in a covered container.

½ pound tofu
½ cup plain yogurt or buttermilk
Juice of 1 lemon
1 small clove garlic
½ teaspoon dry mustard
1 teaspoon tamari soy sauce or miso
Yolks of 2 hardboiled eggs
1 teaspoon chopped tarragon
1 teaspoon chopped chives
1 teaspoon (or more, to taste) capers

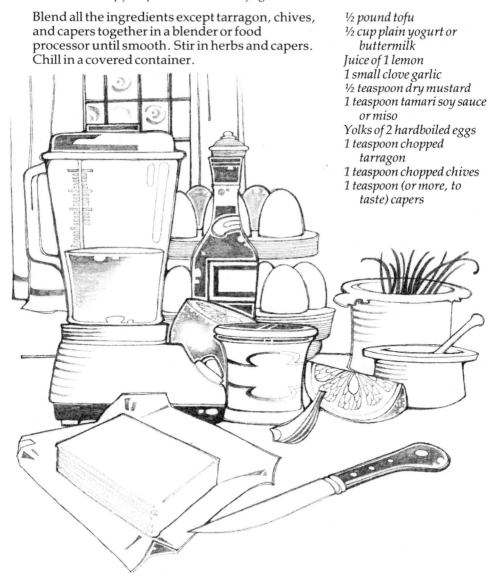

HONEY-LEMON SALAD DRESSING

2 tablespoons lemon juice
1 tablespoon mild honey
1 teaspoon Dijon mustard
Freshly ground black
  pepper
6 tablespoons safflower or
  vegetable oil

Stir together lemon juice, honey, mustard, and pepper. Whisk in oil. Toss with salad just before serving.

LOW-FAT RUSSIAN DRESSING

This has the same sweet tomatoey taste of a Russian dressing, but it is made with tofu and yogurt instead of mayonnaise, so it has none of the fat. Nor does it have the vast amount of sugar present in ketchup. It makes a fine salad dressing or dip for vegetables.

½ pound tofu
½ cup plain low-fat yogurt
Juice of 1 lemon
½ teaspoon dry mustard
1-2 teaspoons soy sauce, to
  taste
1 large, ripe tomato, peeled
2 teaspoons mild honey
2 teaspoons cider vinegar
⅛ teaspoon ground cloves
Pinch of cayenne
2 teaspoons tomato paste

Blend all the ingredients together in a blender or food processor until smooth. Refrigerate in a covered container for up to 1 week.

HOMEMADE TOMATO KETCHUP

Makes about 1½ quarts

1. Quarter tomatoes and cook over high heat in a large saucepan 30 minutes, stirring occasionally. Measure out a little over 2 quarts of the pulp into a large stainless steel or enameled pot. Add onion, sweet red pepper, garlic, and vinegar and bring to a boil.
2. Tie mustard seeds, allspice, cinnamon, peppercorns, bay leaf, cloves, coriander, and pepper flakes together in a doubled cheesecloth. Add to tomatoes along with honey. Simmer uncovered 1 hour over medium heat, stirring often. Remove cheesecloth bag and squeeze out all the moisture.
3. Purée tomato mixture in a blender, then press through a sieve or put through the fine blade of a food mill. Return to pot and simmer over low heat until mixture is thick enough to mound up slightly on a spoon. It will thicken further upon cooling.
4. Ladle into clean, sterilized jars, leaving ½ inch headspace. Wipe rims and cover with canning jar lids.
5. Put jars on a rack in a kettle half full of boiling water. Add more boiling water to cover the lids by 2 inches. Bring to a hard boil, cover pot, and boil 20 minutes.
6. Remove from boiling water and allow to cool. Let mellow in jars 2 to 4 weeks, and once opened, keep refrigerated. Store unopened jars in a cool, dry place.

4 quarts ripe, fleshy tomatoes
1 onion, minced
½ medium sweet red pepper, minced
2 cloves garlic, minced or pressed
1 cup cider vinegar
2 teaspoons mustard seeds
2 teaspoons whole allspice
1 stick cinnamon, broken up
1 teaspoon whole black peppercorns
1 bay leaf
½ teaspoon whole cloves
½ teaspoon ground coriander
⅛ teaspoon dried red pepper flakes
½ cup mild honey

COARSE-GROUND MUSTARD WITH RED WINE AND GARLIC

It is amazingly easy to make your own mustard, and once you begin you will see how many variations you can come up with. I often make mustards as Christmas gifts. They are always appreciated.

4 heaping tablespoons
   mustard seeds
2 tablespoons red wine
⅓ cup red wine vinegar
¼ cup water
¼ teaspoon ground allspice
½-1 teaspoon mild honey,
   to taste
¼ teaspoon freshly ground
   pepper
½-1 teaspoon minced
   garlic, to taste
1 small bay leaf, finely
   crumbled or ground

1. Combine mustard seeds, red wine, and vinegar in a dish and let stand 3 hours or more.
2. Put mixture into a blender jar or food processor and add remaining ingredients. Purée to a coarse texture.
3. Scrape into the top of a double boiler and stir over simmering water 5 to 10 minutes, or until mixture has thickened somewhat. Scrape into a jar, cool, and refrigerate.

Note: This will keep indefinitely in the refrigerator.

ORANGE-PEACH DRESSING

This goes nicely with fruit salads.

3 dried apricots
Juice of 1 lemon
Juice of 1 orange
1 teaspoon mild honey
1 large peach, peeled
¼ teaspoon dry mustard
¼ teaspoon cinnamon
½ cup plain low-fat yogurt

1. Place apricots in a bowl and pour on boiling water to cover. Let sit 10 minutes and drain.
2. Blend all ingredients, including apricots, until smooth in a blender or food processor. Refrigerate until ready to use.

TARRAGON MUSTARD

1. Combine mustard seeds, white wine or vermouth, vinegar, and 1 teaspoon of tarragon in a bowl and let stand at least 3 hours.
2. Pour mixture into a blender jar or food processor (a blender does a more thorough job, but you will have to start and stop it to stir the mixture) and add remaining ingredients except additional teaspoon of tarragon. Purée as finely as you can.
3. Scrape mixture into the top part of a double boiler and stir over simmering water about 10 minutes. A layer will stick to bottom of the pan, but don't worry; it won't burn as long as you are using a double boiler. Cool, add remaining tarragon, and scrape into a jar. Refrigerate.

4 heaping tablespoons mustard seeds
2 tablespoons dry white wine or vermouth
⅓ cup white wine vinegar
2 teaspoons dried tarragon
⅓ cup water
⅛ teaspoon freshly ground pepper
⅛ teaspoon ground allspice
2 teaspoons mild honey

Note: This will keep indefinitely in the refrigerator.

ORIENTAL SALAD DRESSING

Blend all the ingredients together in a blender, or stir together with a fork or whisk until smooth. This is great with vegetable salads and noodle salads and will last a week in the refrigerator.

2 tablespoons sesame tahini
1 tablespoon mild honey
4 tablespoons vinegar
½ teaspoon grated fresh ginger
1 tablespoon tamari soy sauce
2 tablespoons sesame oil
4 tablespoons water or vegetable stock
3 tablespoons safflower oil
Freshly ground black pepper to taste

WHITE WINE SAUCE

Makes 2 cups

1⅓ cups water
8 cloves garlic, peeled and
    left whole
1 cup dry white wine
Sea salt, to taste
5-6 dried black Chinese
    mushrooms
3 tablespoons butter
3 tablespoons unbleached
    white or whole wheat
    pastry flour
Freshly ground black
    pepper

1. Combine water, garlic, white wine, salt, and dried mushrooms in a saucepan and bring to a simmer. Simmer uncovered 30 minutes. Strain and retain liquid.
2. Discard garlic. Rinse mushrooms, remove their tough stems, and slice caps into slivers. Set aside.
3. Heat butter in a heavy-bottomed saucepan over low heat and stir in flour. Cook, stirring with a wooden spoon, a couple of minutes, and just before mixture begins to brown whisk in hot broth and wine mixture.
4. Continue to whisk over medium heat until sauce thickens. Let simmer over low heat 10 minutes, stirring often. Taste and adjust salt.
5. Add freshly ground pepper, and if you wish, stir in slivered mushrooms (or you can use these in something else). Serve over grains, vegetables, crêpes or soufflés. This can be frozen.

AÏOLI: STRONG GARLIC MAYONNAISE FROM PROVENCE

Makes 2 cups

Using a mortar and pestle:
1. Place egg yolks in mortar and squeeze in garlic through a garlic press. Add salt to taste and blend mixture together with pestle until you have a paste.
2. Combine oils and drizzle in by the tablespoon, stirring vigorously with the pestle after each addition, until all the oil is incorporated and you have a smooth, thick mayonnaise.
3. Add lemon juice and pepper and continue to stir vigorously until mayonnaise is uniform. Note that what might appear as lumps are just little pieces of garlic. Do not be alarmed by how garlicky this is; it's supposed to be.

Blender or food processor Aïoli:
1. Place egg yolks in a blender jar or food processor bowl. Squeeze in garlic through a press. Add salt.
2. Turn on machine and very slowly drizzle in the oil in a thin, steady stream. You may have to stop and start blender occasionally and give mixture a stir.
3. Add lemon juice and pepper and mix well.
4. Refrigerate until ready to serve. Use as a dip with vegetables.

2 egg yolks, at room temperature
5 cloves garlic, peeled
Sea salt, to taste
⅔ cup mild-tasting olive oil
⅔ cup safflower oil (or use all safflower oil)
Juice of 1 large lemon
Freshly ground black pepper

POPPY SEED DRESSING

2 tablespoons lemon juice
2 tablespoons vinegar
2 tablespoons plus 1
   teaspoon mild honey
2 tablespoons poppy seeds
Pinch of sea salt
Freshly ground black
   pepper
2 tablespoons safflower oil
⅔ cup plain low-fat yogurt

1. Stir together lemon juice, vinegar, honey, poppy seeds, sea salt, and pepper. Make sure honey is dissolved, and stir in safflower oil and yogurt. Refrigerate until ready to use.

Note: This will keep for a week in the refrigerator. Use with Red Cabbage and Apple Salad (page 121), and crated Carrot Salad (page 119).

PIQUANT TOMATO SAUCE

Makes 1 quart

3 pounds tomatoes, fresh or
   canned, puréed
1 tablespoon olive or
   safflower oil
2 large cloves garlic,
   minced or put through a
   press
½-1 teaspoon crushed
   dried red pepper
1 tablespoon chopped fresh
   basil or 1 teaspoon dried
Sea salt, to taste

1. Purée tomatoes coarsely in a food processor, blender, or through a food mill.
2. Heat the oil in a large, heavy-bottomed saucepan or frying pan and gently sauté the garlic until it begins to colour — 1 or 2 minutes.
3. Add the remaining ingredients and bring to a simmer. Cook uncovered over moderate heat, stirring occasionally, for 20 to 30 minutes.
4. Adjust salt. Serve with pasta, omelettes, vegetables or grains. This can be frozen.

GARLIC TOFU MAYONNAISE

Makes 1¼ cups

1. Combine all ingredients in a blender or food processor and blend until completely smooth.
2. Refrigerate in a covered container. Use as a salad dressing or in place of mayonnaise as a dip or spread.

2 tablespoons lemon juice
2 tablespoons wine or cider vinegar
2 cloves garlic, minced or put through a press
1 teaspoon Dijon mustard
½ cup plain low-fat yogurt
½ pound tofu
2 teaspoons soy sauce
Pinch of cayenne
1 tablespoon safflower oil

CREAMY GARLIC SAUCE

Serves 6

1. Combine garlic, water, bouillon cube, sage, and thyme in a saucepan and simmer uncovered 30 to 40 minutes.
2. Remove from heat and purée in a blender until smooth. Add yogurt and mix well.
3. Stir in parsley, salt and pepper to taste, and if you wish, some lemon juice. Serve with vegetables or grains.

15 cloves garlic, peeled and left whole
1 cup water
1 vegetable bouillon cube
Pinch of thyme
Pinch of sage
1 cup plain yogurt
2 tablespoons chopped fresh parsley
Sea salt and freshly ground black pepper, to taste
Fresh lemon juice (optional)

MILD VINAIGRETTE

Serves 6

Juice of 1 lemon
1 tablespoon vinegar
1 small clove garlic, puréed
  or put through a press
½ teaspoon Dijon mustard
  (optional)
¼ teaspoon tarragon
¼ teaspoon basil or
  marjoram
Sea salt and freshly ground
  black pepper, to taste
½ cup safflower oil, olive
  oil, or a combination

1. Stir together lemon juice, vinegar, garlic, optional mustard, herbs, salt, and pepper.
2. Whisk in oil. Toss with salad of your choice.

YOGURT VINAIGRETTE WITH GOAT CHEESE

Serves 6

Juice of ½ lemon
2 tablespoons red wine
  vinegar
1 small clove garlic, minced
  or put through a press
½ teaspoon Dijon mustard
Sea salt and freshly ground
  black pepper, to taste
½ cup crumbled goat
  cheese
½ cup plain low-fat yogurt

1. Mix together lemon juice, wine vinegar, garlic, mustard, salt, and pepper.
2. Add goat cheese and yogurt and mix well. Toss with salad of your choice.

GARLIC VINAIGRETTE

Serves 4

1. Combine vinegar, garlic, mustard, herbs, salt, and pepper and mix well.
2. Stir in oil and blend well. Toss with salad just before serving.

2-3 tablespoons good wine vinegar
2 cloves garlic, puréed or put through a press
1 teaspoon Dijon mustard
1 teaspoon fresh chopped herbs, such as tarragon, basil, thyme, parsley, marjoram or teaspoon dried tarragon and marjoram
Sea salt and freshly ground black pepper, to taste
⅓ cup good virgin olive oil

VINAIGRETTE MADE WITH GARLIC VINEGAR

Serves 4

This is a much milder vinaigrette. Rather than including fresh garlic in the dressing itself, keep a bottle of wine vinegar on hand in which 1 to 3 cloves of garlic, cut in half, have been submerged for at least a day and preferably longer. Follow the above recipe, omitting the crushed garlic. You may also substitute lemon juice for some of the vinegar.

9

BREADS AND SPREADS

DILL AND COTTAGE CHEESE CASEROLE BREAD

Makes 1 loaf

4 tablespoons lukewarm water
1 tablespoon active dry yeast
1 teaspoon honey
1 cup large curd cottage cheese, at room temperature
1 egg, at room temperature
1 tablespoon grated onion
2 tablespoons safflower oil
1½ teaspoons sea salt
¼ teaspoon baking soda
3 tablespoons chopped fresh dill
¼ cup soy flour
2 cups whole wheat flour
½ to 1 cup unbleached white flour

1. Dissolve yeast and honey in warm water in a large mixing bowl and allow to sit 10 to 15 minutes, or until it bubbles.
2. Press cottage cheese through a sieve, or purée in a food processor fitted with the steel blade. Stir into yeast mixture, and beat in egg. Add onion, oil, salt, baking soda, dill, and soy flour and stir well.
3. Gradually stir in the whole wheat flour. Place about 2 handfuls of unbleached flour on kneading surface and turn out dough. Knead 5 to 10 minutes, adding more unbleached white flour as necessary. Knead until dough is fairly smooth and elastic; it should spring back when indented with fingers.
4. Shape dough into a loaf and butter a loaf pan. Place dough in it, seam side up first, then seam side down. Brush top of loaf with melted butter or safflower oil. Cover and let rise in a warm, draft-free spot until doubled in bulk, about 1½ to 2 hours.
5. Ten to 15 minutes before the end of the rising time preheat oven to 375°F. Bake bread 35 to 40 minutes, or until it sounds hollow when you tap it. Remove from the pan and cool on a rack.

HOLIDAY CHALLAH

Makes 2 braided loaves

1. Scald milk and cool to lukewarm.
2. Dissolve yeast in lukewarm water, and when milk has cooled to lukewarm, stir in along with honey, vanilla, mace, cardamom, eggs, and orange rind. Add 3 cups of the unbleached white flour, a cup at a time, to make a sponge. Stir 100 times, cover, and set in a warm place 1 hour.
3. When hour is up, fold in oil or butter and sea salt, then wheat germ and whole wheat flour. When dough comes away from sides of bowl, place a cup of unbleached white flour on your kneading surface and turn out dough. Knead until dough is stiff and elastic and somewhat silky, adding more unbleached white flour as necessary.
4. Wash out bowl, oil, and set dough in it to rise for 1 to 1½ hours.
5. Punch down dough and turn out onto work surface, which you should flour lightly. Knead in currants and walnuts, then divide dough into 6 equal pieces for 2 braided loaves (or you can make 4 to 6 miniature loaves), weighing the pieces to make sure they are equal. Roll each piece out into a rectangle about 9 inches long, then roll up into a tight cylinder. Roll each cylinder on the work surface until 12 to 14 inches long. Attach 3 cylinders by pinching the ends together. Fold pinched part under and make a braid; pinch together at the other end and fold under. Place braids on an oiled baking sheet and brush with oil. Let rise in a warm place 30 minutes.
6. Towards the end of the rising time, preheat oven to 375°F. Brush braids with egg wash, sprinkle with poppy seeds, and brush with egg wash again. Bake 40 minutes, brushing again with egg wash halfway through. Cool on a rack.

1 cup milk
½ cup lukewarm water
1 tablespoon active dry yeast
3 tablespoons mild honey
1 teaspoon vanilla
½ teaspoon mace
½ teaspoon ground cardamom
3 eggs, beaten
2 tablespoons grated orange rind
4-5 cups unbleached white flour
4 tablespoons safflower oil or melted butter
2 teaspoons sea salt
1 cup wheat germ
2 cups whole wheat flour
½ cup currants
½ cup chopped walnuts
Additional unbleached white flour for kneading
1 egg, beaten with 4 tablespoons water, for egg wash
Poppy seeds

FIG AND WALNUT BREAD

Makes 2 loves

For the dough:
1½ cups milk
6 tablespoons unsalted
    butter
½ cup mild honey
2 scant teaspoons sea salt
2 tablespoons active dry
    yeast
½ cup lukewarm water
2 eggs, at room
    temperature
5 cups whole wheat flour
Up to 3 cups unbleached
    white flour

For the filling:
3 tablespoons honey
3 tablespoons unsalted
    butter
2 teaspoons cinnamon
1 teaspoon ground cloves
1-1½ cups chopped dried
    figs
1 cup finely chopped
    walnuts

For the glaze:
1 egg, beaten with the
    remaining honey-butter
    mixture or with ¼ cup
    water

1. Combine milk, butter, and honey for the dough along with salt in a saucepan and heat together until butter is melted. Stir together to dissolve honey, and set aside until lukewarm.
2. Dissolve yeast in the ½ cup lukewarm water in a large mixing bowl.
3. When milk mixture has cooled, beat in eggs and add to dissolved yeast. Begin stirring in whole wheat flour, a cup at a time. After you have added about 4 cups, stir vigorously 100 times. Add remaining whole wheat flour, fold in, and add a cup of unbleached white flour. By the time you fold this in, the dough should be ready to turn out onto kneading surface.
4. Place some unbleached flour on board and scrape out all the dough. Begin kneading, adding flour as necessary, and knead about 10 minutes, or until dough is stiff and elastic.
5. Oil bowl and place dough in it, rounded side down first, then rounded side up. Cover with plastic wrap or a towel and place in a warm spot to rise for 1½ hours, or until doubled in bulk.
6. Meanwhile prepare your ingredients for the filling. Finely chop walnuts and figs; combine in a bowl. Melt butter and honey together in a small bowl, and stir in cinnamon and cloves.
7. Punch down dough and turn out onto a lightly floured kneading surface. Divide into 2 pieces and knead each into a ball. Let rest 10 minutes.
8. Roll out each piece of dough into a rectangle, about 11 × 8 inches. Brush with honey-butter mixture, then sprinkle with nuts and figs, dividing mixture evenly between the two breads. Leave a 1-inch border around the edge of flattened dough. Roll up dough like a Swiss roll, fold ends in, and pinch all the seams together.

9. Oil breadpans generously and place dough in pans, seam side down. Cover and place in a warm spot to rise 1 hour. Then 20 minutes before the end of the rising, preheat oven to 400°F.
10. Beat egg in bowl in which you melted butter and honey. Brush loaves and place in oven. After 10 minutes turn the heat down to 350°F. Bake another 40 minutes, brushing again with egg wash halfway through the baking. Loaves should be golden brown and respond to tapping with a hollow sound.
11. Remove from heat. To unmold it may be necessary to run a butter knife around the inside edges of the pan. Remove from pans and cool on a rack.

Note: This can be frozen. Once thawed it will dry out fairly rapidly.

BANANA-NUT MUFFINS

Makes 16

1. Preheat oven to 375°F. Butter muffin tins.
2. Sift together flours, baking soda, and spices.
3. Beat together oil, honey, vanilla, and eggs. Stir in lemon rind, mashed banana, and yogurt. Mix well.
4. Quickly stir wet ingredients into dry, along with walnuts. Spoon into buttered muffin tins and bake 20 minutes in preheated oven. Cool on racks, or serve warm.

1 cup whole wheat flour
1 cup unbleached white flour
1 teaspoon baking soda
¾ teaspoon cinnamon
½ teaspoon nutmeg
¼ cup safflower oil
½ cup mild honey
1 teaspoon vanilla
2 eggs
Grated rind of 1 lemon
3 medium bananas, mashed
4 tablespoons plain yogurt
½ cup chopped walnuts

TEXAS CORNBREAD

1 cup stoneground
   cornmeal
½ cup whole wheat flour
½ teaspoon sea salt
1 tablespoon baking powder
½ teaspoon baking soda
1 cup plain yogurt or sour
   milk or buttermilk
½ cup milk
2 tablespoons mild honey
2 eggs
3 tablespoons butter

1. Preheat oven to 450°F.
2. Sift together cornmeal, whole wheat flour, salt, baking powder, and baking soda in a large bowl. Beat together yogurt, milk, honey, and eggs in another bowl.
3. Place butter in a 9 × 9 inch baking pan and place pan in oven for about 3 minutes, or until butter melts. Remove from heat, brush butter over sides and bottom of pan, and pour remaining melted butter into yogurt and egg mixture. Stir together well and fold into dry mixture. Do this quickly, with just a few strokes of a wooden spoon or plastic spatula. It doesn't matter if there are lumps. The important thing is not to overwork the batter.
4. Pour batter into the warm, greased pan, place in oven, and bake 30 minutes, or until top is beginning to brown and a toothpick inserted comes out clean. Remove from heat and let cool in pan. Eat warm or cool, with honey.

MOIST PUMPERNICKEL

Makes 2 loaves

1. Dissolve yeast in lukewarm water and allow to stand until it bubbles. Meanwhile, put oil, caraway seeds, salt, and molasses in a large bowl and pour in milk. Make sure milk is lukewarm and stir in yeast mixture. Stir together well.
2. Stir in mashed potatoes, bran, wheat germ and rye flour, a cup at a time, and mix well. Fold in whole wheat flour a cup at a time. The dough should be coming away from the sides of the bowl before you finish adding the whole wheat flour.
3. Place whatever remains of the whole wheat flour on work surface (use unbleached white if none remains). Turn out dough and scrape out what remains in bowl. Flour hands and begin to knead. The dough will be sticky. Knead 10 to 15 minutes, adding unbleached white flour as necessary, but remembering that the dough remains somewhat sticky. When dough is stiff, oil bowl, form dough into a ball, and place in bowl seam side up first, then seam side down. Cover with a towel or plastic wrap and place in a warm spot to rise until doubled in bulk, about 1½ to 2 hours.
4. Punch down dough and turn out onto a lightly floured board. Knead a few times and divide into 2 pieces, which should weigh about 2½ pounds each. Oil a baking sheet or bread pans and shape into loaves. The dough will be moist. Slash dough with a razor blade or a sharp knife and let rise, covered, 45 to 50 minutes.
5. Toward the end of the rising time preheat oven to 375°F. Place loaves in oven and set timer for 15 minutes. After this time brush with egg wash and sprinkle with poppy seeds. Bake another 30 to 35 minutes, and cool on a rack.

2 tablespoons active dry yeast
½ cup lukewarm water
2 tablespoons safflower oil
2 tablespoons caraway seeds
1 scant tablespoon sea salt
3 tablespoons molasses
2 cups milk, scalded and cooled to lukewarm
2 cups mashed potatoes
1½ cups flaked bran
½ cup wheat germ
2½ cups rye flour
3 cups whole wheat flour
Up to 1 cup unbleached white flour, for kneading
1 egg, beaten with 2 tablespoons water for egg wash
Poppy seeds for topping

Note: This freezes well

RYE-OATMEAL BREAD WITH ANISE AND RAISINS

This is a great breakfast bread.

Makes 2 loaves

For the sponge:
2 tablespoons active dry
  yeast
3 cups lukewarm water
3 tablespoons strong or
  mild honey
3 tablespoons molasses
2 cups unbleached white
  flour
2 cups whole wheat flour

For the dough:
4 tablespoons safflower oil
2 teaspoons sea salt
2 tablespoons crushed anise
  seeds
2 tablespoons grated
  orange rind
2 cups rolled oats
1 cup raisins
2 cups rye flour
1 cup whole wheat flour
Unbleached white flour as
  necessary
1 egg, beaten, for egg wash

1. Make sponge. In a large bowl dissolve yeast in lukewarm water and add honey and molasses. Stir in unbleached flour and whole wheat flour, a cup at a time. When all the flour has been added, stir about 100 times to incorporate well. Cover with plastic wrap or a damp towel and set in a warm place to rise for an hour. By the end of this time it should be bubbling away.

2. Make dough. Fold in safflower oil and salt, then anise seeds and orange rind, then oatmeal and raisins. Fold in rye flour, a cup at a time, and whole wheat flour. By now you should be able to turn bread out onto kneading surface.

3. Flour kneading surface generously with unbleached white flour and scrape out dough. Flour hands, and begin to knead. Knead 10 to 15 minutes, adding unbleached white flour as necessary, until dough is stiff and elastic.

4. Shape dough into a ball, oil bowl, and place dough in it seam side up first, then seam side down. Cover and let rise in a warm place 1 hour.

5. Punch down dough and let rise again, covered, 50 minutes.

6. Now turn onto a lightly floured board, knead a few times, and divide into two equal pieces. Form into loaves and place in oiled bread pans, upside down first, then rightside up. Let rise 15 to 25 minutes, or until loaves rise above edges of pans, while you preheat oven to 350°F.

7. Brush loaves with beaten egg, slash with a sharp knife or razor blade, and bake in preheated oven 50 to 55 minutes, until bread is brown on top and responds to tapping with a hollow, thumping noise. Remove from pans and cool on a rack.

Note: This can be frozen.

ZUCCHINI-CARROT MUFFINS

Makes 24

1. Preheat oven to 375°F. Butter muffin tins.
2. Sift together flours, powdered milk, baking powder, salt, and spices.
3. Beat together eggs, oil, honey, marmalade, vanilla, and milk. Stir in grated carrot and zucchini.
4. Quickly stir wet ingredients into dry, and fold in walnuts. Spoon into muffin tins, filling ¾ full, and bake in preheated oven 20 minutes. Cool on a rack, or serve warm.

1 ½ cups whole wheat flour
½ cup unbleached white flour
4 tablespoons powdered milk
1 tablespoon baking powder
½ teaspoon sea salt
½ teaspoon allspice
½ teaspoon nutmeg
1 teaspoon cinnamon
3 eggs
¼ cup safflower oil
½ cup mild honey
4 heaping tablespoons orange or ginger marmalade
1 teaspoon vanilla
½ cup milk
1 cup grated carrot
1 cup grated zuchini
½ cup chopped walnuts

HERB AND GARLIC BREAD

You can make any of your favorite breads into garlic bread by adding 1 to 2 cloves, sautéed in a little oil, to the recipe. Below is a mixed rye and whole wheat variety that I particularly like. This freezes well.

Makes 1 loaf

1 tablespoon active dry
 yeast
1 cup lukewarm water
1 tablespoon mild honey
½ medium onion, minced
2 cloves garlic, minced or
 put through a press
3 tablespoons safflower or
 vegetable oil
1-1½ teaspoons sea salt
½ cup plain yogurt
2 cups rye flour
1 tablespoon thyme
1 teaspoon sage
4 cups whole wheat flour

1. Dissolve yeast in water in a large bowl. Add honey and set aside 10 minutes. Meanwhile sauté onion and garlic in 1 tablespoon of the the oil until onion is tender, and set aside.
2. When yeast is bubbly, stir in remaining safflower oil, salt, yogurt, and sautéed onion and garlic. Stir in rye flour, a cup at a time, and add thyme and sage. Fold in half, whole wheat flour.
3. Place a cup of remaining flour on kneading surface and scrape out dough. Knead 10 minutes (it will be very sticky at first), adding more flour as necessary.
4. When dough is stiff and elastic, knead into a ball, oil bowl and place dough in it, turning once to coat with oil. Cover with plastic wrap or a damp towel and let rise in a warm place 1 to 1½ hours, or until doubled in bulk.
5. Punch down dough and turn out onto a floured surface. Oil a breadpan. Knead dough a minute or two and form into a loaf. Place in breadpan, seam side up first, then seam side down.
6. Cover and let rise in a warm place 45 minutes, or until dough reaches top edge of pan. Meanwhile preheat oven to 375°F.
7. Bake in preheated oven 45 to 50 minutes, or until brown and the loaf responds to tapping on the bottom with a hollow sound.
8. Remove from pan and cool on a rack.

OATMEAL, CORNMEAL, AND HONEY BREAD

Makes 2 loaves

1. Dissolve yeast in water in a large bowl. Stir in honey and yogurt, and gradually whisk in the first 2 cups unbleached white flour, then the first 2 cups whole wheat flour. Stir 100 times, then cover bowl with plastic wrap or a damp towel, and place in a warm spot to rise for 1 hour, or until bubbling.
2. Fold in salt and oil, then oats and cornmeal. Begin adding whole wheat flour, and when you can turn dough out of bowl place a cup of flour on your kneading surface and turn out dough. Knead 10 minutes, adding flour as necessary. When dough is stiff and elastic, oil bowl and place dough in it seam side up first, then seam side down. Cover and leave in a warm place to rise 1 to 1½ hours, or until doubled in size.
3. Punch down dough and turn out onto a floured surface. Knead a few times, then divide dough in half and form 2 loaves. Place in oiled breadpans, upside down first, then rightside up, cover, and set aside to rise 1 hour, or until bread comes above edges of pans. During the last 15 minutes of rising, preheat oven to 375°F.
4. Lightly brush loaves with beaten egg, place in oven, and bake 45 to 55 minutes, or until golden and they respond to tapping with a hollow sound. Remove loaves from oven and pans and cool them on a rack.

2 cups lukewarm water
1 tablespoon active dry yeast
1 cup plain yogurt
4 tablespoons mild honey
2 cups unbleached white flour
2 cups whole wheat flour
1 tablespoon sea salt
4 tablespoons safflower oil
2 cups rolled oats
1 cup cornmeal
2 cups whole wheat flour
Additional 2 cups whole wheat or unbleached white flour for kneading*
1 egg, for glaze

If your flour is very coarse and heavy, use unbleached white flour or find a lighter whole wheat pastry flour.

Note: This bread freezes well. Double wrap in plastic wrap and foil or plastic wrap and a plastic bag.

WHEAT GERM AND FRUIT MUFFINS

Makes 15

1 cup unbleached white
   flour
1 tablespoon baking powder
½ teaspoon sea salt
1 teaspoon ground
   cinnamon
½ teaspoon allspice
1 cup toasted wheat germ
2 eggs
⅓ cup melted butter
3 tablespoons mild honey
2 tablespoons brandy
1 teaspoon vanilla
1 cup milk
1 cup chopped fresh fruit,
   such as peaches, apples,
   pears, or berries

1. Preheat oven to 375°F. Butter muffin tins.
2. Sift together flour, baking powder, salt, spices, and wheat germ.
3. Beat together eggs, butter, honey, brandy, vanilla, and milk. Quickly stir into dry ingredients. Fold in fresh fruit.
4. Spoon into muffin tins and bake 20 minutes in preheated oven. Cool on a rack, or serve warm.

LEFTOVER GRAINS MUFFINS

This is a great way to use up last night's cooked grains. The
texture will vary depending on what grains you use.
Cooked brown rice yields a chewy, hearty muffin; bulghur,
couscous, and millet yield a lighter, moister muffin.

Makes 15

1. Preheat oven to 400°F. Butter muffin tins.
2. Place dried apricots or figs in a bowl and cover with boiling water. Let sit 5 to 10 minutes.
3. Sift together flour, baking powder, and sea salt.
4. Beat together eggs, honey, melted butter, milk, and almond extract. Stir in cooked grains.
5. Drain fruit, squeeze out water, and chop.
6. Quickly stir wet ingredients into dry, and fold in chopped dried fruit. Spoon into muffin tins.
7. Bake 20 minutes in preheated oven. Cool on a rack, or serve warm.

½ cup chopped dried
  apricots or figs
1¼ cups whole wheat flour
2 teaspoons baking powder
½ teaspoon sea salt
2 tablespoons mild honey
¼ cup melted butter
2 eggs
⅔ cup milk
½ teaspoon almond extract
1 cup cooked brown rice,
  millet, couscous,
  bulghur, or other grains

ORANGE-DATE MUFFINS

Makes 18

1 cup whole wheat flour
½ cup unbleached white flour
2 teaspoons baking powder
½ teaspoon salt
½ cup wheat germ
2 oranges
½ cup milk
¼ cup melted butter
2 eggs
½ cup mild honey
½ cup chopped dates

1. Preheat oven to 375°F. Butter muffin tins.
2. Squeeze enough juice from oranges to make ½ cup. Combine with milk. Take one of the squeezed oranges and chop coarsely. Place chopped rind in a blender with milk, butter, eggs, and honey and blend until finely chopped.
3. Stir wet mixture into dry ingredients and quickly mix together. Fold in dates. Spoon into prepared muffin tins and bake 20 minutes in preheated oven. Cool on a rack, or eat warm.

Note: These can be frozen.

MORNING TOFU SPREAD

This is nice to have on hand to spread on toast in the morning.

½ pound tofu
¼ cup plain yogurt
2 small apples
2-3 tablespoons mild honey
2 tablespoons lemon juice
½ teaspoon cinnamon
¼ teaspoon nutmeg
1 tablespoon sesame tahini
½-1 teaspoon vanilla, to taste
2 teaspoons whole wheat pastry flour

1. Preheat oven to 350°F and bake apples until completely soft. Core apples and set aside.
2. Oil or butter a loaf pan or 1-quart casserole. Keep oven on.
3. Blend all ingredients including baked, cored apples together until completely smooth in a blender or food processor and pour into prepared baking dish. Bake 30 to 40 minutes, or until firm and just beginning to brown. Cool and refrigerate. Spread on bread or toast.

Note: This will last a week in the refrigerator, well wrapped.

WHITE BEAN AND BASIL SPREAD

Serves 6

1. Combine basil and garlic in a blender or food processor or in a mortar and grind them together until you have a fairly smooth paste.
2. Add white beans and tahini and blend until smooth. Add salt and lemon juice to taste, and freshly ground black pepper. Chill.
3. Serve on croûtons or bread. This can be frozen but is better fresh.

1 cup fresh basil
2 large cloves garlic
1 cup raw white beans, cooked
2-3 tablespoons tahini, to taste
Sea salt, to taste
Juice of 1 lemon (more or less, to taste)
Freshly ground black pepper

HERBED CHEESE SPREAD

This should burst forth with the flavors of spring. You can omit some of the herbs if you wish, or substitute others. Use whatever is available.

1. Using a wooden spoon or mixer, combine all the above ingredients, mixing well. You can also use a food processor for this, but you must be sure to use a plastic blade and not a steel one, or your herbed cheese will become green.
2. Refrigerate until ready to use. Serve as a spread or as a dip. Very nice party fare.

Note: This will keep for two days in the refrigerator.

½ pound either Ricotta or cream cheese
4 tablespoons chopped fresh basil
4 tablespoons chopped fresh parsley
2 tablespoons chopped fresh marjoram
1 tablespoon chopped fresh thyme
3 tablespoons chopped fresh chives
Juice of ½ lemon
Sea salt and freshly ground black pepper
1 clove garlic, pressed or puréed

FINES HERBES BUTTER

4 ounces unsalted butter
1 small clove garlic, minced
    or puréed (or pressed)
1 teaspoon minced shallot
1 teaspoon minced chives
1 teaspoon minced fresh
    thyme
1 tablespoon minced fresh
    parsley
1 tablespoon minced fresh
    basil or tarragon
Sea salt to taste

1. Chop herbs finely. Let butter come to room temperature and blend in herbs.
2. Transfer to a mold or an attractive butter dish and refrigerate. Soften slightly before serving.

PEANUT BUTTER-TOFU SPREAD

Safflower oil for baking
    dish
½ pound tofu
5 tablespoons plain low-fat
    yogurt
3-4 tablespoons mild
    honey, or to taste
1 large or 2 small bananas
2-3 tablespoons unsalted
    peanut butter, to taste
½ teaspoon cinnamon
½ teaspoon nutmeg
1 teaspoon vanilla
1 tablespoon lemon juice
2 teaspoons whole wheat
    flour

1. Preheat oven to 350°F. Lightly oil a small baking dish or a 1-quart casserole.
2. Blend all the ingredients together until smooth. Pour into baking dish and bake 30 to 40 minutes, or until firm and just beginning to brown. Remove from oven, cool, and chill.

Note: This will keep for a week in the refrigerator. It does not freeze.

10

DESSERTS

PEAR CLAFOUTI

Serves 6

1. Combine honey, lemon juice, and liquor. Place pears in a bowl and cover with alcohol mixture. Let sit 1 hour, tossing from time to time to marinate evenly.
2. Place milk, honey, eggs, vanilla, and salt in a blender and turn it on. Add flours while blender is running. Blend for 1 minute. If mixing by hand, blend together eggs and flour with a wooden spoon and whisk or beat in liquids. Strain through a fine strainer. Let batter rest 30 minutes.
3. Preheat oven to 350°F. Drain pears and add 6 tablespoons of their marinating liquid to batter. Butter a 2-quart flameproof baking dish and pour in a ¼-inch layer of batter. Place over a moderate flame 1 to 2 minutes, or until a film has set on the bottom. Now spread pears in a layer and pour on remaining batter.
4. Place in preheated oven and bake 45 minutes, or until puffed and brown and a knife plunged into the center comes out clean. Serve hot or warm, with a little cream or yogurt to moisten if you wish.

1 tablespoon mild honey
Juice of ½ lemon
4 tablespoons either sweet white wine, eau de vie de poires, or Kirsch
1½ pounds firm, ripe pears, peeled, cored, and sliced

For the batter:
1 cup milk
2 tablespoons mild honey
3 eggs
1 tablespoon vanilla
Pinch of sea salt
6 level tablespoons unbleached white flour
6 level tablespoons whole wheat pastry flour
6 tablespoons liquid from the pears
Yogurt or cream for topping

PEAR-ALMOND TART

Serves 8

For the crust:
*¾ cup whole wheat pastry
   flour*
*¾ cup unbleached white
   flour*
Pinch of sea salt
½ cup ground almonds
4 ounces unsalted butter
¼ teaspoon vanilla
½ teaspoon almond extract
1½ tablespoons mild honey

For the glaze:
1½ cups red wine
2 tablespoons lemon juice
2 tablespoons mild honey
1 stick cinnamon
1 teaspoon vanilla
*1½ pounds ripe pears,
   peeled, cored, and
   quartered*
*1 tablespoon cornstarch
   dissolved in 1
   tablespoon water*

For the rest of the tart:
½ lemon
1½ pounds firm ripe pears
¼ cup blanched almonds

1. First make crust. Mix together flours, salt, and ground almonds and cut in butter. Add vanilla and almond extract and honey. The dough should come together like a normal, yet sticky, pie dough. If it is very crumbly add a teaspoon or more of ice-cold water. Wrap and chill one to two hours.
2. Preheat oven to 375°F. Roll out pie crust and line a well-buttered 10-inch tart pan or pie dish with dough. The dough may be very crumbly when you roll it out. It might help to roll it out between pieces of waxed paper. Just persevere and patch it together if it falls apart.
3. Line tart shell with a sheet of aluminum foil and weight with ½ lb of dried beans. Bake 6 minutes in preheated oven. Remove lining and prick pastry shell in several places. Bake another 8 to 10 minutes, or until lightly browned. Cool on a rack.
4. Combine red wine, lemon juice, honey, cinnamon, and vanilla in a 2-quart saucepan and bring to a simmer. Simmer 5 minutes and drop in pears intended for glaze. Simmer 20 to 30 minutes. Remove cinnamon stick and purée pears through a food mill or in a blender. Return to poaching liquid and continue to cook over medium high heat until mixture is cooked down to 1½ cups. Dissolve cornstarch in a little water and add to purée, stirring. Turn down heat and simmer until mixture becomes a nice glaze, which should take only a minute or two.
5. Fill a bowl with water acidulated with the juice of ½ lemon. Peel and core remaining pears, cut into quarters, and drop into water. Drain carefully.

6. Pour all but ½ cup of the pear-wine purée into pie crust and spread evenly. Place pears over purée like petals of a flower. If they will not lie flat slice a flat edge along the bottom. With a very sharp, stainless steel knife cut thin slices across each quarter. Place 3 blanched almonds in each space between petals, and the remaining almonds in the center. Spread remaining glaze evenly over the pears with a pastry brush. Serve.

PUMPKIN CAKE

1. Have all ingredients at room temperature. Preheat oven to 350°F and place rack in the lower half. Butter a bundt pan or a 10 × 4½-inch tube pan. If using a tube pan line with buttered waxed paper.
2. Sift together flour, baking soda, baking powder, spices, and sea salt. Add a tablespoon of the sifted dry ingredients to raisins in a small bowl, and toss with optional nuts to coat. Set aside.
3. Beat together honey and oil until creamy. Beat in pumpkin purée, then eggs, one at a time. Add rum. At low speed beat in dry ingredients, a cup at a time, scraping the sides of the bowl well. Beat only until smooth. Stir in raisins and nuts.
4. Turn into prepared pan and bake 1 hour and 5 minutes, or until a cake tester comes out dry. Cool on a rack for 10 minutes or so. Cake will only fill the pan ¾ full. Invert onto a rack, remove pan, and cool. Serve with whipped cream flavored with vanilla and rum.

3 cups sifted whole wheat pastry flour
2 teaspoons baking soda
2 teaspoons baking powder
1 tablespoon cinnamon
½ teaspoon powdered ginger
¼ teaspoon powdered cloves
¼ teaspoon nutmeg
¼ teaspoon allspice
¾ teaspoon sea salt
1 cup raisins
1 cup broken walnuts (optional)
1 cup mild, medium, or strong honey
1 cup safflower oil
2 cups cooked, puréed pumpkin
5 eggs
3 tablespoons rum
Butter for the pan
Whipped cream

CAROB SPONGE ROLL

Even chocolate addicts (who always hate carob) have to admit that this is outstanding. It really does taste like chocolate. I think it's the combination of the coffee and carob chips.

Oil or butter for the baking pan
6 ounces carob chips or solid bar
2 teaspoons instant coffee, dissolved in 6 tablespoons hot water
8 large eggs, separated
Pinch of sea salt
½ cup mild honey
4-8 tablespoons carob powder, to taste
1 cup whipping cream
2 tablespoons mild honey
1 teaspoon vanilla
2 tablespoons Kahlua

1. Preheat oven to 350°F. Oil or butter a jelly roll pan and line it with waxed paper, with a 2-inch overhang on each end to serve as handles.
2. Dissolve carob nuggets or bar (break into pieces) in coffee in a small pan over low heat.
3. Beat egg yolks with a pinch of salt and honey at high speed in an electric mixer until mixture is very thick and somewhat stiff. Beat in carob-coffee mixture.
4. In a separate bowl beat egg whites with a pinch of salt until they form soft peaks. Be careful not to beat them too stiff, or you'll have trouble folding them into carob mixture. Stir ¼ of the beaten egg whites into egg yolk-carob mixture, then gently fold in remaining egg whites, or gently fold lightened egg yolk mixture into the whites, depending on which bowl is bigger.
5. Pour this mixture into prepared jelly roll pan and gently spread it evenly all over the surface. Bake in preheated oven 20 minutes, or until firm to the touch.
6. Dampen a dish towel or a length of 4 paper towels folded in half. When you pull the sponge out of the oven cover it immediately with the damp towel, and place a dry towel or length of paper towels over this. Let dessert roll cool, covered thus, until baking sheet is cool enough to handle.
7. Loosen sides of roll with a knife. Sprinkle top with carob powder. Place two lengths of waxed paper over top of sponge, and holding ends firmly, quickly reverse sponge roll and remove baking sheet. Now carefully remove waxed paper.

8. Beat cream in a chilled bowl until fairly stiff and add additional honey, vanilla, and Kahlua. Beat a little more. When sponge is cool enough so that it won't melt whipped cream, place dollops of cream all around the edges and spread all over the surface in a thick even layer.
9. Using the ends of the waxed paper as handles, and placing a board or platter, whatever you will be serving the roll on, at one edge of the roll, carefully roll up sponge lengthwise like a jelly roll, up onto serving surface. Cover with plastic wrap or waxed paper, and refrigerate until serving time, or freeze and thaw 15 minutes before you wish to serve.

Note: When you roll the sponge, don't be alarmed if it tears a little. It won't fall apart.

PINEAPPLE-BANANA MINT SHERBET

Serves 4

1. Blend orange juice and mint together in a blender until mint is very finely chopped, or liquified. Blend in remaining ingredients, except garnish, and purée until smooth.
2. Pour into ice trays or a baking dish and freeze until just beginning to set. Remove from freezer and beat with an electric mixer, a whisk, or in a food processor to break up ice crystals. Place in freezer again and repeat once more when just beginning to set.
3. Pack into a container and freeze. If frozen solid, let soften in refrigerator 1 hour before serving. Serve garnished with fresh mint.

½ cup orange juice
2 tablespoons fresh mint, plus additional for garnish
1 large, ripe pineapple, peeled, cored, and coarsely chopped
1 tablespoon fresh lime juice
2 tablespoons mild honey
1 large ripe banana

APPLE SOUFFLÉ WITH CALVADOS

Serves 4 to 6

1 tablespoon butter
2 tablespoons wheat germ
1½ pounds cooking apples,
   peeled, cored, and
   halved
1⅓ cups water, acidulated
   with the juice of ½
   lemon
6 tablespoons mild honey
½ teaspoon cinnamon
⅛ teaspoon freshly grated
   nutmeg
2 teaspoons cornstarch
1 additional tablespoon
   lemon juice
3 tablespoons Calvados
6 large egg whites, at room
   temperature
¼ teaspoon cream of tartar
Pinch of sea salt

1. Preheat oven to 425°F about 15 minutes before baking. Butter a 2-quart soufflé dish and dust with wheat germ. Refrigerate while you prepare soufflé mixture.
2. Slice half of 1 of the apples thinly. Place ½ cup of the acidulated water in a heavy saucepan, bring to a simmer, and poach apple slices 3 to 4 minutes. Drain and set aside.
3. Chop remaining apples fine and place in a medium saucepan with another ½ cup of the acidulated water and 1 tablespoon of honey. Bring to a simmer and cook uncovered 30 to 35 minutes, or until thick. Stir in cinnamon and nutmeg.
4. Combine remaining water and honey in a medium saucepan and bring to a boil. Boil 5 minutes and add to apple mixture. Bring to a simmer, stirring.
5. Dissolve cornstarch in remaining tablespoon of lemon juice and stir into apple mixture. Heat thoroughly, stirring, until nice and thick, about 5 minutes. Remove from heat, transfer to a mixing bowl, and stir in Calvados.
6. In another clean, dry mixing bowl beat egg whites until they begin to foam. Add cream of tartar and a pinch of salt. Continue to beat until egg whites form stiff shiny peaks. Do not overbeat. Whisk ¼ of the egg whites into apple purée, combine thoroughly, and gently fold in rest.
7. Gently spoon soufflé mixture into prepared dish. It should come just about up to the top. Sprinkle poached apple slices over the surface and place immediately in preheated oven. Bake 16 to 17 minutes, or until well browned. Remove from oven, and serve at once.

BLUEBERRY TART

Serves 8

1. Preheat oven to 350°F. Prebake pie crust 5 minutes. Remove from heat and turn oven up to 450°F.
2. Toss together berries, lemon juice, and honey. Dissolve cornstarch in the Crème de Cassis and toss with berries. Turn into pie crust.
3. Place tart in oven and bake at high heat 10 minutes, then turn heat down to 350°F, and bake another 20 to 30 minutes, or until crust is nicely browned. Remove from heat and cool on a rack.

1 tart crust of your choice (pages 166 and 172)
1½ pounds blueberries
Juice of ½ lemon
3 tablespoons mild honey
1 tablespoon cornstarch
3 tablespoons Crème de Cassis liqueur

PEARS POACHED IN BEAUJOLAIS WITH PEPPERCORNS

Serves 6

1. Peel pears, leaving stems intact.
2. Combine Beaujolais, honey, and peppercorns in a saucepan and bring to a boil. Drop in pears, reduce heat, and simmer 15 minutes, or until the outside of pears is translucent but pears are still firm. Remove from the heat and allow to cool, then chill several hours. Should be served very cold.

6 comice pears
1 bottle Beaujolais
½ cup mild honey
2 tablespoons whole black peppercorns

ALMOND-GRANOLA PIE CRUST

½ cup ground almonds
½ cup either rolled oats,
  granola, or muesli
1 cup whole wheat pastry
  flour
1 teaspoon ground
  cinnamon
¼ teaspoon sea salt
4 ounces unsalted butter
1-1½ tablespoons mild
  honey

1. Mix together ground almonds, oats, granola or muesli, whole wheat flour, cinnamon, and salt. Cut in butter. Add honey and gather into a ball.
2. Butter a tart pan and rather than rolling out the crust, press into pan. Fill pan by pressing portions of the dough from the center of the pan out flat with your fingers. Cover entire pan and pinch an attractive edge round the rim.
3. Refrigerate 1 to 2 hours and prebake 5 minutes at 350°F before filling.

HONEY-POACHED PEARS

Serves 4

2 cups dry white wine,
  preferably a Chablis or
  Chardonnay
½ cup mild honey
1 teaspoon vanilla extract,
  or ½ vanilla bean, split
2 tablespoons lemon juice
4 firm ripe pears
1 tablespoon chopped fresh
  mint

1. Combine white wine, honey, vanilla, and lemon juice in a non-aluminum saucepan and bring to a boil. Reduce heat and maintain at a simmer.
2. Peel, quarter, and core pears and drop immediately into simmering wine. Simmer 15 minutes. Drain and pour liquid back into saucepan.
3. Boil down wine for about 10 minutes, or until you have about a cup and it is thick and amber colored.
4. Place pears in a serving bowl and pour in wine. Serve warm or chilled, garnished with mint. These can be refrigerated overnight.

LEMON-WALNUT WAFERS

These are delicate, sweet, and tart. They are somewhat brittle.

Makes 36

1. Preheat oven to 350°F and adjust 2 oven racks to divide oven into thirds. Butter baking sheets.
2. Sift together flours, baking powder, salt, and ginger and set aside. Cream butter with honey. Add egg and egg yolks and beat until mixture is light and fluffy.
3. On low speed gradually add dry ingredients, scraping bowl and beating only until mixture is smooth. Beat in vanilla, lemon juice and rind, and stir in nuts.
4. Drop by rounded teaspoons onto biscuit sheets, 2 to 3 inches apart, as they spread. Bake 18 to 20 minutes, reversing sheets halfway through baking. The wafers do not brown on the tops, but they do around the edges. Cool on racks.

¼ cup sifted soy flour
1¼ cups sifted whole wheat pastry flour
½ teaspoon baking powder
¼ teaspoon sea salt
⅛ teaspoon ground ginger
4 ounces butter
1 cup mild honey
1 egg plus 2 egg yolks
3-4 tablespoons lemon juice, to taste
Finely grated rind of 1 large lemon
½ teaspoon vanilla extract
½ cup walnuts, broken into medium pieces

PUMPKIN PIE

1 dessert pie crust (pages
  166 or 172)
3 eggs
1 pound cooked, puréed
  pumpkin
1 cup milk
2 tablespoons butter
½ cup strong honey
1 tablespoon molasses
1 ½ teaspoons vanilla
  extract
2 teaspoons ground
  cinnamon
½ teaspoon ground ginger,
  or 1 teaspoon fresh,
  grated
¼ teaspoon mace
¼ teaspoon ground cloves
¼ teaspoon freshly grated
  nutmeg
1 tablespoon rum
¼ teaspoon sea salt
Whipped cream or plain
  yogurt

1. Preheat oven to 350°F. Roll out pie crust and line a 10-inch pie pan or tart pan. Beat 1 of the eggs and brush pie crust, then prebake 7 minutes. Remove from oven and turn up heat to 425°F.
2. Blend remaining eggs with rest of ingredients except whipped cream or yogurt. Pour into pie shell. Bake 10 minutes, then reduce heat to 350°F, and bake another 30 to 40 minutes, or until firm to the touch.
3. Cool and serve with whipped cream or plain yogurt.

BROWN RICE PUDDING

Serves 4 to 6

1. Preheat oven to 325°F.
2. Beat eggs together with sea salt, milk, and honey. Stir in vanilla, lemon peel, lemon juice, the spices, raisins, apples, and the rice.
3. Place in a buttered 1½- or 2-quart baking dish or soufflé dish and bake 50 minutes in preheated oven until set. Serve warm or cold, topped with yogurt.

3 eggs
Pinch of sea salt
1½ cups milk
½ cup mild honey
1 teaspoon vanilla
2 teaspoons grated lemon peel
1 tablespoon lemon juice
½ teaspoon cinnamon
¼ teaspoon ground nutmeg
½ cup dark or golden raisins
2 apples, cored and chopped
2 cups cooked brown rice
Plain low-fat yogurt for topping

CHAMPAGNE SORBET

Serves 4

¾ cup mild honey
⅔ cup water
Grated rind of 2 oranges
Grated rind of 1 lemon
1 quart freshly squeezed
   orange juice, strained
Fresh juice of 1-2 lemons,
   to taste, strained
1 bottle champagne, not too
   dry
½ cup Grand Marnier
Strawberries and mint for
   garnish

1. In a heavy-bottomed saucepan dissolve honey in water and simmer with orange and lemon peel 20 minutes.
2. Strain and add to orange and lemon juice, along with champagne and Grand Marnier. Stir well and freeze in ice-trays or a sorbettier. If using ice-trays, blend with an electric mixer or food processor halfway through the freezing to break up the ice crystals.
3. Let soften in refrigerator 30 minutes before serving if frozen solid. Serve garnished with strawberries and fresh mint.

A GLOSSARY OF HERBS

ANISE

Anise has a distinct liquorice flavor. Its leaves, which look a bit like chervil leaves, bright green and feathery, can be added to salads and cooked vegetables for a nice variation. Its seeds are an important ingredient in spice breads and cakes, and in some biscuits. The herb is an annual that can grow to a height of 2 feet. It likes light, fertile soil and lots of sunlight and heat.

BASIL

I have friends in Texas who are so addicted to basil that they devote an entire garden every spring to this special herb. I envy them this garden, for I must settle for a small windowpot — although I can find generous bunches daily in my market — and I am almost as fanatical about it as they. It is, I think, my favorite herb. Known in France as "l'Herbe Royale" (its name derives from the Greek "basilikon", which means royal), it was made to accompany tomatoes and pasta, to season Mediterranean vegetable dishes, and will gladly find its way into egg, grain, and cheese dishes, salads, and curries (it grows abundantly in India). It has a pronounced sweet and pungent flavor and is sometimes rather peppery. There are a few varieties of the plant. Most familiar are those with the large, dark green leaves. In the South of France the basil plants are bushy, with very small green leaves; these have a stronger, more anisey flavor than the larger leaf plants. There is also a beautiful variety with purple leaves.

The ultimate basil preparation is *pesto* (page 138) in Italy, *pistou* in Provence. This is a paste made with large quantities of basil, which is ground together with garlic, pine nuts (for pesto), olive oil, and cheese (Parmesan and Romano in Italy, Gruyère or Parmesan in France). Pesto is served with pasta or vegetables, and Pistou is stirred into a thick mine-strone-like soup just before the soup is served.

Common or sweet basil is an annual and can grow to about 3 feet high. It should be started after all danger of frost is past. It grows well in pots and needs lots of sunlight and moisture. If you keep picking off the flowers once they begin to appear, your basil will last well into the fall.

In France you will often see basil in pots on restaurant terraces. This is because basil is known to ward off flies, which are annoyingly abundant and persistent in Provence. It has always been a tradition for farmers to give the plants as house gifts. A welcome gift indeed, but in my house it wouldn't last very long as an insect repellent.

BAY LEAVES

Since antiquity the "Noble Laurel" has been reputed to sharpen the wit of the poet and strengthen the powers of the prophet. It has always symbolized victory on the battle fields and playing fields, and for almost as long its virtues as a culinary herb, just as important, have been widely recognized. The oil of the waxy, dark green leaves of the bay laurel imparts a distinct herbal flavor to soups, stews, vegetable, and bean dishes. I remember vividly the first time I was aware of this taste: I was served lentil soup for the first time at a friend's house, and adored it. I asked my friend's mother what the seasoning was, and she said it was bay leaf. I went right home and requested lentil soup made with bay leaf in it, and have used this herb ever since in stocks, bean dishes, marinades, and many soups. Bay leaves add a rich, subtle flavor to slowly cooked vegetables like artichokes and eggplant. They are an important element in marinades, partly because of their anti-bacterial properties.

BOUQUET GARNI

A *bouquet garni* consists of one or two sprigs of thyme, one or two sprigs of parsley, and a bay leaf, tied together. Sometimes a stalk of fennel is also included, depending on what you are using it for. It is indispensable in vegetable stocks and stews, imparting a subtle herbal flavor.

CARAWAY

Caraway, known for its distinctly flavored seeds, is one of those herbs that people either like or detest, so it's best not to serve a dish seasoned with caraway to guests whose tastes are unfamiliar to you. I grew up eating Jewish rye bread with caraway seeds and have always loved the flavor. Not only does it go beautifully with rye, but it is great in potato soups, grain soups, and various salads. Used judiciously it will not dominate a dish but will accent it in a very interesting way. The plant is a biennial and likes sandy soil and full sunlight.

CAYENNE

Although often considered a spice, cayenne and the other members of the Capsicum family (the chilis and paprikas) are herbs. It is very high in vitamin C and has several medicinal properties. I take a capsule of it whenever I feel a cold coming on, and it invariably works as a preventative. In the kitchen a small pinch will heighten the flavor of a dish and make something special out of what otherwise might have been a good but not exceptional pot of beans, a soup, or vegetable dish. And not because you and your guests have burnt your mouths. You should be careful never to add too much cayenne, for it is among the hottest of peppers. A pinch is usually sufficient.

CHERVIL

Chervil has been my most exciting herb discovery since coming to live in France in 1981. Nothing can mimic its sweet, pungent flavor. It is a delicate, feathery plant, a little like flat-leaf parsley in appearance but lighter in color and more fern-like. Its leaves should never be chopped, but plucked from the stems, because chopping bruises the herb and alters its fine, refreshing flavor. Whole strands of chervil add distinction to salads, and the leaves make a particularly elegant garnish for soups, vegetables, eggs, and sauces. It is high in vitamin C and iron and is known to stimulate the appetite.

Chervil is a hardy biennial that grows best when sown in late summer in well-drained, light soil. It will do well in half shade and in window boxes.

CHIVES

These look like tiny scallions and are the mildest member of the onion family. A hardy perennial, they are easy to grow, require partial sun and any kind of soil, and should be kept around the kitchen so you can snip them into salads and soups, omelettes and sauces, lightly cooked vegetables, potatoes, herb butters, and fresh cheeses. A lowly pan of scrambled eggs becomes quite special with the addition of chives (page 28). They are high in vitamin C and are one of the *fines herbes*, with chervil, parsley, and tarragon.

CORIANDER
(or **CILANTRO**)

This is a herb I discovered in Mexico, where it is a common ingredient in all sorts of dishes. It is another one of those herbs people either love or hate, and I am someone who loves its strong taste. I first discovered it in the best bowl of beans I'd ever eaten, in a large family restaurant in a Mexican border town. Since then I've never made beans without it; I'm hooked. Mexican or Tex-Mex hot sauce is another food item that cannot exist without cilantro (fresh coriander). I later discovered that this herb is a frequent ingredient in Chinese dishes and curries. It is easy to find in Oriental markets.

Coriander has never been easy for me to grow because it goes to seed very quickly. It likes full sun and chalky soil.

Coriander seeds, whole or ground, have an altogether different flavor. They are an important seasoning in Greek-style marinated vegetables and ground in curries, spice cakes, and breads. Their flavor is slightly musty and spicy.

CUMIN

This is considered by some to be a spice, but I have found it listed in more than one herbal. It has a distinctive, spicy-earthy flavor and is indispensable in curries, many Mexican dishes, and many Middle Eastern dishes. It goes well, whole or ground, with certain cheese and vegetable creations, with potatoes and tofu, and with beans of all kinds. I like it very much with lentils, and I often make a bread seasoned with the whole seeds when I am serving Mexican food.

When I lived in Austin, Texas, I had a huge dill plant in my front yard that I didn't plant. It was right next to the garbage can, and a seed must have been dumped there and germinated. How lucky I was. I was forever using the versatile herb for my dinners, where I would season different versions of cucumber soups and salads, soups, potato dishes and cabbage dishes and breads with the dill, whose unique, fresh flavor cannot be duplicated.

Dill is widely used in Eastern European and Scandinavian cooking. For that reason I associate it with dishes containing yogurt, cucumbers, potatoes, and cabbage. It is an annual that can grow to a height of about 3 feet, and it looks very much like wild fennel, with tall, hollow stalks and feathery, green leaves. The flavors of the two are not at all similar, however, but they like to cross-pollinate and should never be planted close together.

Dill will grow like a weed from seed, but it must have a well-drained, rich soil and abundant sunshine to thrive.

Dill seeds have a much stronger, saltier flavor than the leaves. They are slightly similar to caraway, though not as strong. I like to add them to breads and cheeses and to tofu spreads, and when ground they make a good salt substitute.

Fennel is one of the earliest known herbs. It was discovered in ancient times that it aided in the digestion of oily fish, thus the herb was and still is widely used in fish cookery. Among the Greeks it had the reputation of making fat people lean, and it has always been famous for its good effect on the skin and the eyes.

The anise-flavored, feathery-leafed plant looks like dill and grows like a weed in warm climates. I have seen it on canyon roads in Los Angeles, all over Provence, and along the coast in Britain. Cultivated fennel likes full sun and well-drained soil.

Chopped fresh fennel is a refreshing addition to salads and vegetable dishes and makes a fine garnish for some soups. I like to add it to quiches, and use it sometimes in omelettes and cheese dishes. The seeds are much like anise in flavor, and find their way into Greek-style marinated vegetables, some breads and soups, and other braised vegetable dishes.

FINES HERBES

The *fines herbes* consist of parsley, tarragon, chervil, and chives. Use them in omelettes, cream sauces, cheese spreads, quiches, and salads. Adding *fines herbes* to a dish is like adding a touch of springtime.

MARJORAM and OREGANO

Marjoram and oregano come from the same family. Oregano is often referred to as "wild marjoram", and indeed, it has a stronger, more rustic flavor.

Marjoram has a minty, somewhat thyme-like flavor (it is also called "sweet marjoram"), and is great in salads, soups — especially of the minestrone variety — pizzas, pasta, and vegetable dishes. It is a half-hardy, bushy annual that cannot withstand frost. Its leaves are small, plentiful, and silver-green. The flowers are knotty and purplish and appear at the top of the stem. They have a strong aromatic scent. The plant can grow to a height of 3 feet and is easy to cultivate in pots and window boxes.

Oregano is more rustic than marjoram and more widespread in southern Europe, where it is found growing wild all over the sunny hillsides. It looks like marjoram but has a stronger, more peppery odor. It too will grow to a height of 3 feet and can be cultivated in pots and window boxes. It likes very well-drained, light soil and lots of sun.

I associate oregano first and foremost with Italian food. A pizza wouldn't be a pizza without it. It was one of the first herbs I ever used, because spaghetti sauce was one of the first things I ever learned to make, and my mother instructed me to add oregano to it. The herb is equally important in many Greek bean dishes and salads, as well as Mediterranean vegetable dishes, eggplant dishes, and hearty soups.

MINT

There are numerous varieties of mint, but the ones used most often in cooking are spearmint and peppermint. I also use apple mint, which has a milder flavor, and pennyroyal, whose tiny leaves are strong and peppery. The recipes in this book are best suited for peppermint.

Once you begin to explore North African and Middle Eastern cuisines you will see how versatile this herb is. It is widely used in these regions in salads, grain dishes, vegetable dishes, and soups. Mint changes the entire aspect of a dish, but used judiciously it will not overpower the other ingredients. The effect is a refreshing one. I often garnish fresh fruit with mint. A tablespoon or two can pick up something as simple as a bowl of sliced oranges and make a really special dessert out of them. It adds an elegant touch to berries, melon, and peaches, too, and blended into fresh orange juice it will make a breakfast drink that will open your eyes much more effectively than a cup of coffee.

Mint grows easily from cuttings in well-watered soil or in pots. It does not need or even like direct sunlight, and requires a good deal of moisture. It spreads quickly, so contain it with bricks or rocks if growing it in your garden. The herb is a very hardy annual.

PARSLEY

This is the herb with which we are most familiar. The eternal garnish, parsley can go much further than that. It has a slightly bitter flavor and goes well, alone and in combination, with other herbs, with vegetables, grains, legumes, pasta, cheese, and eggs. Middle Eastern and North African recipes often call for large quantities of parsley and here it is quite distinguishable. You find it in abundance in salads, grain dishes, egg dishes, and vegetable and legume combinations.

Parsley is an effective antidote for garlic and onion breath, so serve it with dishes highly seasoned with these ingredients.

The herb comes in several curly varieties, which are what we most often see at supermarkets and greengrocers. But the flat-leafed Italian parsley is actually preferable, for it has a richer, cleaner, more pronounced fragrance. A hardy biennial, it can grow to a height of 2 feet and is easy to cultivate in pots and window boxes. The seeds take a while to germinate. It likes shade and rich, well-worked soil.

ROSEMARY

This is one of the strongest of the herbs. Its resinous, spiky leaves impart a pungent, savory flavor to Italian and Provencal vegetable dishes, to broiled foods and marinades, where its anti-bacterial properties are as important as its gastronomic virtues. The herb is an evergreen shrub that grows all over

Provence and Italy. Because it's so easy to come by in these regions, when I am there I am always adding it to tomato sauces, ratatouilles, vegetables, and bean dishes. The plant can grow to a height of 5 feet and likes light, sandy, fairly dry soil and either full or partial sunlight. It gives off a spicy aroma. I prefer the fresh herb to the dried, not just because of its flavor, but because the leaves of dried rosemary are hard and spiky.

Rosemary seems to have more legends attached to it than any other herb. It goes back thousands of years. It was considered a symbol of immortality by the Greeks and Romans, and was favored for its powers of rejuvenation by the court of Louis XIV.

Rosemary's medicinal virtues are well documented. As an infusion it is a tonic and digestive, stimulating the liver function and circulation. It is excellent for the skin and hair, and its oil makes an effective liniment for sprains, bruises, and gout.

SAGE

Another herb with a very distinctive flavor, a little sage goes a long way, and can really make a dish. I shall never forget the spinach and ricotta gnocchi finished in sage butter, which I ate for lunch one day at a small Florentine restaurant. The sage added that special stunning touch that made this dish a truly memorable one. The herb often finds its way into Italian dishes like tomato sauces and slowly simmered vegetable dishes. It is good with pumpkin (a remarkable northern Italian speciality is a pumpkin ravioli with ground almonds, parmesan, and sage), eggplant, and potatoes.

Sage often becomes moldy and takes on an unappetizing musty flavor when dried, so be very careful if drying the herb yourself, and make sure you buy the herb from a reliable source. Dried, it is quite good in stuffings and herb breads.

The plant is a kind of shrub, with thick, long, slender leaves, grey-green, with a pebbly texture. It likes well-drained soil and lots of sunlight.

Sage tea is a good tonic and blood purifier, and the herb is reputed to ensure a long life. The name, in fact, comes from the Latin word *salvare*, to save. Numerous proverbs have been written about its attributes. A Provencal maxim goes:

Sage Saves
He who has it in his garden
Has no need of medicine.

SUMMER SAVORY

This is known as "the bean herb" in America, and in the South of France it is used frequently to season fresh goat cheeses. It lends a delicate flavor to beans of all kinds, fresh or dried, and is also used in aromatic sauces. Rather than adding a different flavor of its own, like coriander or cumin, it brings out the flavors of the foods it is cooked with. In this way it makes an excellent substitute for salt.

Summer savory is a bushy annual that can grow to a height of about 1 foot with sparse, dark green leaves along the stems. It likes full sunlight.

One of the reasons that savory has traditionally been added to bean dishes is that it aids in digestion. It has also always had a reputation as an aphrodisiac (its name derives from "satyrus"), which may account for its popularity.

SORREL

Sorrel is considered both a vegetable and a herb. Used widely in France in soups and purées, alone and with other vegetables, it has been sadly neglected in the United States and Britain. It has a strong acidic flavor, very distinctive and somewhat metallic due to its high oxalic acid content. It should never be cooked in aluminum or metal pots because it oxidizes easily. Sorrel is not only excellent in soups and sauces, but also in egg preparations like omelettes and *oeufs cocottes*.

The leaves of the sorrel plant are broad, oblong, and dark green. They look a little like flat spinach leaves. The plant is very high in vitamins A and C and in iron. It grows well in light, rich soil and in full sunlight. Combine it with spinach, lettuce, and other greens in soups, salads, and purées. It has a strong flavor and a little goes a long way.

When you cook sorrel it will turn a brownish-green color upon contact with the heat. The first time I worked with it I kept pulling out leaves, thinking I'd overlooked some bad ones while washing them. When they all turned the same color I realized that this must be normal.

TARRAGON

French tarragon (avoid Russian tarragon, which is flavorless) is one of the most luxurious of the herbs. Its long, narrow leaves have a unique sweet flavor, somewhat like basil but more tangy, somewhat like anise but not as liquoricey and more bitter. It is very aromatic, essential in Sauce Béarnaise, and is one of the *fines herbes* always welcome in omelettes, quiches, salads, and herb butters and cheeses. A few tablespoons of freshly chopped tarragon will turn an ordinary vegetable broth into a truly elegant soup, perfect for the first course of a rich meal, and even less will make something very special out of a salad.

Tarragon can never be grown from seeds but must be started from cuttings or purchased as small plants. The leaves are bright green and widely spaced on thin stems. The plants need full sun and well-drained soil. The herb is excellent with delicate vegetables like asparagus, peas, and artichokes, and in light cream sauces. It makes a delicious aromatic vinegar and is marvelous, even in its dried state, in vinaigrettes. This is a very useful herb for salt-free diets.

THYME

Thyme is another one of my favorite herbs. I couldn't be without it, not just for the *bouquet garni* it must be part of, for seasoning soup stocks, beans, and sauces, but for the distinct, tangy touch its tiny green leaves add to vegetable and cheese dishes, soups, and salads. It is so distinguishable that a little goes a long way, and it is because of this unmistakable flavor that I love it so much. It is delicate and earthy at the same time. Dried thyme is an important ingredient in herb breads and bean pâtés, and also savory bean dishes and soups.

Garden thyme can grow to about 12 inches and is a perennial evergreen bush. Lemon thyme is a creeper and is most suitable in rock gardens. Like rosemary, it grows all over Provence and Italy, and I grew accustomed to running out and picking it for one dish or another every time I cooked when I lived in the South of France.

The thymes like chalky, fertile soil and full sunlight. They spread quickly.

INDEX